HUMAN
ENCOUNTERS
and
KARMA

Ana Rezende-Missir.

HUMAN ENCOUNTERS and KARMA

by
ATHYS FLORIDE

translated by
CHRISTOPHER BAMFORD

ANTHROPOSOPHIC PRESS

This book is a translation of *Les Rencontres Humaines et le Karma*, published by Editions Anthroposophiques Romandes, 11, rue Verdaine, 1204 Genève/Suisse, 1983. Translation made by permission of the author.

Les Rencontres Humaines et le Karma ©1983
Editions Anthroposophiques Romandes

Library of Congress Cataloging-in-Publication Data

Floride, Athys.
   [Rencontres humaines et le karma. English]
   Human encounters and karma / by Athys Floride: translated by Christopher Bamford.
   Translation of: Les rencontres humaines et le karma.
   Includes bibliographical references.
   ISBN 0-88010-291-8
   1. Anthroposophy.   2. Interpersonal relations — Religious aspects.
3. Karma   4. Reincarnation.   5. Hugo, Victor, 1802–1885 — Miscellanea.
I. Title.
BP596.I57F4613   1990
299'.935—dc20
            90-45625
            CIP

This translation © 1990 Anthroposophic Press
Published by: Anthroposophic Press
RR 1, Box 94 A-1
Hudson, New York 12534

Book design and production by Studio 31

Printed in the United States of America

Table of Contents

PART TWO
ENCOUNTERING A POET THROUGH HIS WORK

Dedicated
to all those
who wish to go further
in their encounters

Foreword

Knowledge of the laws of karma and reincarnation is becoming increasingly important. The new age of light, which human beings entered at the end of the Kali Yuga, urgently demands of us an awareness of the living reality of karma, which must be understood as penetrating even the facts and details of daily life.

A consequence of this is a greater awareness of one of the most characteristic events of human life: the meeting of human beings with each other. Such meetings do not occur arbitrarily at the whim of "chance," but reflect, hidden beneath a veil, the realities of karma.

The new spiritual path of karma demands that we awaken to what is veiled and unveiled in these encounters and participate consciously in the processes that bring them about. We can no longer remain passive before this person or those persons but must ask: Why is this meeting taking place? What does it mean in my life? How can I become fully conscious of a bond with this person or that? Such questions can only receive answers through the inner activity of those taking part in the meeting. We must become, more and more, collaborators in this area. This is what the new spirituality, the new Light, asks of us.

PART ONE

HUMAN ENCOUNTERS and KARMA

Introduction

*No religion exists yet. If you believe religion to be possible,
it must be made and brought forth out of the union of
several individuals.*

Novalis

What is an encounter with another human being? What
does such a meeting mean for a person's life? What is
revealed when two or more people meet together? What is
the connection between an encounter and the knowledge of
karma and destiny?

Questions like these arise when we become interested in
meetings between people. We have the powerful feeling that
we're touching on an intimate matter involving not only
human beings, but other beings, especially the gods, as well.
Is not every meeting in fact a moment in the evolution of
humanity as well as of the gods? Is not every meeting actually
a critical moment in the world's evolution? After all, we
know that it is human beings who make history, and who
thereby also shape the evolution of the world. Such are some
of the questions that we shall try to shed light on here.

Human encounters can be looked at from different points
of view. We could, for instance, adopt the scientific point of
view and proceed as follows: "Suppose a young person — not
an infant, but someone who's already about fourteen — is
asked to solve consciously the problem of how to make a
decisive encounter with another person occur when he or
she is fifty years old. Just imagine what a problem it would
be — what an effort it would take — if you had to solve this
by calculation, like a problem in arithmetic!" [1] In this example Rudolf Steiner draws our attention to the enormous
complexity involved in human encounters; and he adds that

the first hierarchy must apply the highest mathematics or resort to science to solve so difficult a problem. Steiner states: "Even the superficial details of human life can be fitted into calculable laws."

We could also consider human encounters from an artistic point of view: people meeting each other then would act like artists, freely forming the substances born between them. In this book, however, we will deal with human encounters from the point of view of religion.

In pre-Christian times, science and art were the prerogative of the temple and the priesthood. The evolution of the human spirit, however, successively liberated first science (thanks, for example, to Socrates, Plato, and Aristotle) and then art (thanks to Giotto), placing these activities more and more in the hands of particular human beings, free individualities. Today it would seem to be the turn of religion to realize itself in daily life. We shall try to show here that religion has not become decrepit and dried up, but has been placed in the hands of each one of us, so that our task is now to cultivate it responsibly and knowledgeably. This knowledge can be deepened by the study of anthroposophy, which can make us conscious of perspectives that will renew the experience of encounter.

From the religious point of view every meeting between people includes three basic stages:

1. the period before the encounter
2. the encounter itself
3. the period after the encounter

This is the structure that we shall adopt in order to illuminate this most important part of human life. In the course of our existence, each of us meets innumerable other human beings. Some of these meetings are brief, evanescent, others are more important, some are decisive. Some are limited to a look, a casual word in the street, others take on dimensions that transform our lives.

To conclude, let us note that we find in human biography, without our being conscious of it, the activities of science, art, and religion. That is to say, human biography completely fulfils what anthroposophy aspires to, namely, the reunion of these three great domains. Our task is to become conscious of them by penetrating them with our cognitive powers.

I

From Before the Encounter
Up To the Encounter

Anyone who views life other than as an illusion that consumes itself is still entangled in life. Life should not be a novel given to us, but one written by us.

Novalis

A human being in the physical world structures space in such a way that we can distinguish a center and a periphery. At the center is the human being, while at the periphery is everything that the person perceives by means of the senses. When the person moves, this spatial configuration moves along with him or her.

Everything that appears in this space, arising within it through the senses, is more or less clearly perceived. Human

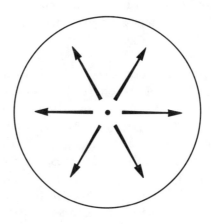

encounters also take place here. As long as a second person has not yet appeared within this circle (see diagram), no encounter has taken place. This does not mean that the first person has no connection to the second, but only that the connection has not yet penetrated to a conscious level. However, the forces that will bring about a meeting between the two are already at work.

In his lecture of January 25, 1924, on the two gates of the Sun and the Moon, Rudolf Steiner described how lunar and solar forces penetrate and work in human lives. Lunar forces surround human beings with an iron necessity; solar forces grant them the possibility of freedom. Before people meet each other, before they find each other in earthly life, they have worked on each other without knowing it.

> If two people meet, let us say, when one is twenty and the other twenty-five, they can look back on everything they have experienced up to that point. It will become clear to each of them that every single detail in their lives has been urging them on towards this meeting. Both the twenty-year-old and the twenty-five-year old can look back over their lives and see how they came from different directions to meet each other in this particular place. In shaping our destiny, everything depends on two people setting out from two different parts of the globe and then meeting as if brought together by an iron necessity directing them towards the point in which they meet.[2]

Before two people meet, they are led toward each other by necessity; and the point where they meet lies within the space I have mentioned. As soon as the two people perceive each other within this space, as soon as their circles interpenetrate, something remarkable happens: they enter their field of mutual vision, and solar forces begin to work.

Is there an event in human history which illustrates an important encounter and confirms Rudolf Steiner's description? The Baptism in the Jordan gives us a primordial image. First, John the Baptist and Jesus of Nazareth, both of whom

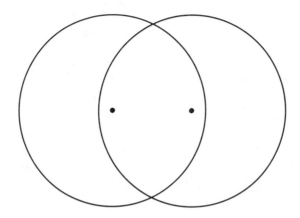

belonged to the Hebrew lunar culture, met. Then the Baptism was performed, allowing the solar forces to bind themselves with the being of Jesus. The forces of necessity, of Jehovah, had penetrated Hebrew culture and sternly led this people. Within it, St. John and Jesus unfolded their destinies to the point of their historic meeting. Then the moon gave way to the sun, to the impulse of freedom for humanity. And we can see how after this important meeting the forces of the moon, which had guided these two great spirits with the hand of necessity, had to diminish, while the forces of the sun, the Christ forces, had always to increase. The words of John the Baptist — "He must increase but I decrease" — take on quite another resonance, and seal the universal nature of this meeting. Ancient, lunar karma must be transformed, metamorphosed by means of the forces of the sun, of Christ. These must undergo dying and becoming, sacrifice. For this reason John the Baptist was beheaded while the I of Jesus made way for the solar God. All of humanity can see this meeting at the turning point of the ages as an archetypal image, a model, and a source of life.

The question arises: How can this powerful impulse be realized on the level of the individual in daily life? It seems to me that here lies a task having to do with the liberation of religion. Rudolf Steiner deals with the question in his lecture *The Work of the Angels in Man's Astral Body*. He draws attention to the fact that human encounters will become more and more of an enigma and that we must learn to approach others with an ever-deepening interest.

Yes, there will come a time when human beings will not be able to live as though asleep, but will receive an impulse to action from the spiritual world through their angels. This impulse will demand that they develop a much deeper interest for every human being, deeper than we can imagine today. This heightened interest in our fellow human beings will not simply be something subjective that people can develop comfortably and at leisure, but will happen all of a sudden. The spiritual world will instill in human beings a sense of the specific mystery of what the other person is. I mean this very concretely, and not just as some kind of theoretical consideration. People will experience something of interest to them in each and every other human being.[3]

When the destinies of two people (the action of the lunar forces) bring them face to face, each one of them is at a specific stage in his or her biography. Since a biography never stops developing, this means that a process is set in motion between the two people. Then it is a question of giving a different meaning to daily life, of cultivating our meetings with others from another perspective, with different intentions; in a word, it is to live daily life religiously.

A being can help us in this task — he of whom Rudolf Steiner said in his last address, "His magical and poetic idealism enables him to resurrect even the most insignificant material thing and let its spiritual glory shine forth."[4] This being is the poet Novalis.

There is only one Temple in the world and that is the human body. There is nothing more sacred than this higher form.

Novalis

II

Religion and Daily Life

During the Encounter
First Stage: The Proclamation

Our whole life is an act of worship.
In ordinary life, we serve like priests at the altar.

Novalis

Meeting another person can be a double experience. On the one hand, we may find ourselves confronted with forces from the past; then again it may be that we must prepare ourselves for some future task. In any event, a future task for each of us must be to know ourselves and work in harmony with evolution, that is, to realize what we really want through this encounter, what we ourselves have decided upon before birth.

The moment of encounter can become a sacred moment in our lives if we try to put into effect something Rudolf Steiner spoke about when he said: "In the future each human being will see the divine concealed in every other human being." And "In the other human being, a revelation from the divine foundations of the world presents itself to us in flesh and blood." [5]

Such knowledge of oneself and the other may be discovered in the course of a process:

1. learning to know each other outwardly;
2. gaining a deeper insight into the being of the other person;

3. recognizing the karmic forces at work in the encounter, through which

4. a new stream of forces comes about.

Let us consider this evolutionary process. We become aware that people participating in a meeting in this way experience something which otherwise takes place during divine service, during the Mass. We know that the Mass unfolds in four main stages:

1. Proclamation;
2. Sacrifice (Offertory);
3. Transubstantiation; / Transformation - points Toward future.
4. Communion.

To awaken in this way to what really happens between two or more people who meet each other — to perceive in depth the unfolding of an encounter — is to turn Rudolf Steiner's prediction into reality in our daily life:

> Any truly religious feeling developing within human-kind in the future will be based on recognizing the image of the divinity in every human being as a matter of immediate daily experience, and not merely in theory. There will be no need to force people to be religious because then, right from the onset, every meeting of person with person will be a religious act, a sacrament.[6]

Here the gods' intention is clearly expressed: religion, the connection between human beings and the gods, is to become a free act, an intentional activity leading to the cultivation in daily life of a conscious bond with the spiritual world. For "at the source of angelic impulses lies the intention to pour out over human beings the possibility of complete freedom in religious activity."[7] That is true esotericism. It is our task, even our obligation, not to sleep through this reality. Awakening in our encounters in this way, we are on the way to performing the same sacrament as that of the Mass.

When someone appears in our field of perception we feel the need to know who this person is. This is the first stage: an exact knowledge of who this person is on the physical plane. A being is announced, full of mystery: Who is it? We see him or her for the first time. What secret does he or she bear? We learn the person's name and where he or she comes from; we learn something about the outer circumstances of the person's real life in his or her present incarnation. The stage can appear banal; it is often seen this way; but there is nothing banal about it. We should not forget Rudolf Steiner's words:

> The first stage in the formation of a human community is when we awaken to the outer appearance of another person. Usually we are asleep before the other. How can we wake up? We awaken thanks to the outer world — its light, sound, warmth — thanks to all that comes to us from the world of the senses. We awaken also — at least in our daily life — through the outer, natural appearance of other human beings.[8]

This statement makes it clear how important our sensory perceptions are. Therefore let us develop this attention and interest for the outer appearance of our neighbor. Faced with our neighbor, we are usually inattentive and dreamy, with little interest in this side of his or her being. This is why it is often difficult to remember these outer appearances. But we have been given our senses in order to perceive, and in order to perceive ever more consciously. When another human being enters the circle of our perceptions, we are not permitted to go on dreaming, but must wake up to who he or she is physically.

This attention to the other sets in motion the four-stage process we are considering. The powers of destiny, human forces, have sent me this person whom I see on the physical plane. An event in my destiny announces itself. At the moment when I meet him or her, the solar forces begin to work, bringing freedom. What will become of this meeting? How will it continue? What will I make of it? All this is no longer subject to necessity. I must take hold of this instant of freedom, I must live this first stage consciously. From now on it is up to me to decide to guide this process through the next three stages.

III

The True Image
of the Human Being

Second Stage: The Sacrifice (Offertory)

I am Thou.

Novalis

Human beings are immersed in the flow of evolutionary time. As soon as we are born, we enter into the quality of change. Only death ends this situation; until then human beings never cease to become. Thus we are faced with the following questions: How can we take part consciously in this becoming? Is it altogether possible? We have seen how in the moment of meeting, when our partner enters the circle of our perceptions, the solar forces, the forces of freedom, begin to work. The hour of freedom rings out. What does this mean? Nothing less than the possibility of participating consciously from that moment on in the evolution of the relationship born of the encounter.

Once the first stage has been completed, a space has opened toward the future. We can feel the need to go further on the path, to deepen this new connection. But of course the process can also be broken off at this point, either because the person we met disappears from our lives or because, not noticing the importance of the moment, we do not seize it consciously, we let it slip away. It is comforting to know that usually the forces of destiny bring us together again and again, until eventually we wake up. But if we take hold of the process deliberately and consciously, we are ready to take a second step that will lead to a deepening of the connection with the other person.

25

However, there is a condition attached to taking this step. How are we to pass beyond the veil of the physical? How can we enter more deeply into the other? A sacrifice becomes necessary. We must be able to open and give ourselves devotedly to whatever seeks to show itself in the encounter. Many are those who, unconsciously renouncing any deepening of the relationship, remain at the first stage and are satisfied with a purely external bond. Such people shut themselves off, as it were, from the inquiring gaze of the other. "Hell is other people": here fear, indifference, egotism are in full command.

The second step, the stage of the offertory, as we would like to call it, is taken only with difficulty. There is no doubt that one could go further and open oneself devotedly to the other. Indeed, when the ego has been sacrificed on the altar of encounter, something important happens. By virtue of this sacrifice, the true image of the other arises to the one who has sacrificed him or herself. The external, physical, natural aspect, which one came to know with such interest during the first stage, is overcome; it is no longer an obstacle. "What, then," we ask, "is the true image of this human being?"

At this point we need to heed a warning from Rudolf Steiner. As a general rule, people do not perceive each other with sufficient awareness. The usual reaction — simply to find the other person sympathetic or unsympathetic — is superficial; for the existential human condition is to be thrown into the conflict between the opposing forces of Lucifer and Ahriman.

In former times, pagan peoples lived in myths, in a world of images, while the Jewish people strove toward abstraction in the form of the Law. Steiner therefore warns us to "put aside our current way of looking at things with its remnants of 'Thou shalt not make any graven images' and find our way back, this time consciously, to the soul's old image-forming capacity."

In the future, it will only be possible to organize society appropriately by means of images and imaginations. . . . The next opportunity to restructure society will depend on our ability to apply consciously the same strength that was present, unconsciously or only semiconsciously, in the old myth-making ability of the human race. . . . Once people have arrived at this <u>pictorial ability</u>, this conscious myth-making, through their worldview, the possibility will be opened for social forms to evolve out of interactions between human beings.[9]

The quotation that follows can be taken as an exercise in developing this capacity of approaching the true image of the human being, as required by the spirit of our time.

If you look at an image such as this statue of the Representative of Humanity with Lucifer and Ahriman on either side,[10] you are face to face with what is actually at work in each human being as a totality, because human beings are in fact in the state of balance between the Luciferic and Ahrimanic forces. If the impulse to confront people in this way, to concretely see this trinity in each individual, permeates your daily life, then you will begin to understand your fellow human beings. It is essential that we cultivate this ability now in the fifth post-Atlantean epoch, so that we do not just continue to pass each other by like ghosts, defining each other by means of our abstract concepts without being able to form any images of each other. What we do now is nothing more than pass each other by as if we were ghosts. One ghost comes up with the thought, "That person's a nice fellow," the other, "That person's not such a nice fellow": "that's a bad man," "that's a good one" — just a lot of abstract concepts.[11]

But what do people want in the depths of their being? What do they want to accomplish?

The fact is, as Steiner says, that an image "radiates out from deep within each human being, an image that expresses the person's unique state of balance. When two people come face to face, each one should perceive the image welling up out of the other." But in order for this to happen, we must "develop the heightened interest I have often described to you as the basis of human society, the powerful interest each human being should feel when in the company of another human being."[12]

In Rudolf Steiner's lecture cycle, *The Mission of the Archangel Michael*, we find the epistemological basis for this perception or image that we seek to find in the other:

> We must learn to look at people as they will be in the future, that is, to think Michaelically. Let me describe this Michaelic thinking more precisely. Although you may not be saying it out loud or even thinking it, in the intimate depths of your consciousness you're saying to yourself, "This is a person of flesh and blood, an earthly material human being." But you don't really see the actual being who pulls this material together. The right train of thought would be, "I see before me particles of matter accumulated by a spiritual human form in order to make this invisible being visible." Real human beings are actually invisible. If in every waking moment we are fully conscious of this fact, and cease to regard a human being as the conglomerate of mineral particles he or she arranges in a particular way, then we are thinking Michaelically. To know that we are in the company of invisible human beings — that's what thinking Michaelically means.[13]

Another of Rudolf Steiner's exercises also helps in this second stage. This exercise asks of those who would practice it a great love of and trust in the other. Steiner calls it the way to Christ through thinking:

> Instead of taking an interest merely in my own way of thinking, and in what I consider right, I must develop a selfless interest in every opinion I encounter, however strongly I may hold it to be mistaken. The more people pride themselves on their own dogmatic opinions and are interested only in them, the further removed they are from Christ at this moment in world evolution.

People must develop a brotherly, social interest in the opinions of others, even if they think they're mistaken. They must allow the opinions of others to shed light on their own thinking and take the same interest in the possibly mistaken thoughts of others as they do in thoughts of their own which they hold to be true. The more they're able to do so, the more they'll feel in their soul of souls one of Christ's sayings, which today must be interpreted in the sense of the new Christic language.

Christ said, "Inasmuch as ye have done it unto the least of these my brethren, ye have done it unto me." The Christ never ceases to reveal Himself anew — even unto the end of earthly time. And thus He speaks today to those willing to listen: "In whatever the least of your brethren thinks, you must recognize that I am thinking in him; and that I enter into your feeling whenever you bring another's thought into relation with your own, and whenever you feel a fraternal interest for what is passing in another's soul. Whatever opinion, whatever outlook on life, you discover in the least of your brethren, therein you are seeking Myself."[14]

At the first stage we saw that a lack of interest could hinder us from truly awakening to the physical appearance of the other, to his or her natural aspect. Similarly, at the second stage, we must avoid being so in love with our own thoughts and opinions that we are unable to be objective about them. If we take up allowing ourselves to be permeated through and through with the opinions and thoughts of another, sacrificing our own opinions for the moment, as a spiritual exercise or path, then the other person can express what he or she is.

Everything that the other person expresses in words emanates from that person and may be thought of as a substance radiating toward us. When this is so, we become a vessel for the other: we create a free space for the other's being. To do this is to perform a sacrifice, but through this sacrifice some of the obstacles between human beings may be overcome, leaving the way open for the next stage.

IV

Destiny:
Perception of the Forces of Karma

Third Stage: Transubstantiation

We will understand the world once we understand our-
selves, since we and it are integral halves of the same
whole. We are God's children, divine seeds. At some point
we will become as our father is.

Novalis

Receiving another person's thoughts into oneself and letting
them unfold within one's own soul prepares one to attempt
the next stage. This stage, which corresponds to the Transubstantiation, must be willed; to do so will take all the strength
we possess. The perception of the other, of the true image
of the other, of our bond with the other, now becomes
deeper. We enter the realm where the forces of karma are
at work. Now we can strive to understand the impulses, the
currents bringing us together with other human beings.

The previous stage, which we called the stage of sacrifice,
corresponds to the Offertory. It allowed us to open ourselves
up to another being coming toward us. Yet a certain mystery
still remained — the reasons for this meeting. Why has this
person come to me? What aspect of our past unites us?
What will we have to do together in the future?

In order to get to the bottom of this mystery, to lift the
veil of Maya, we must allow forces to work in us that will
transform us so completely that they let us see beyond the
bounds of our present incarnation. These forces are solar
forces that have united themselves with the earth, the solar

forces of Christ Jesus, which are connected with karma. They are the forces that bring freedom, and we must individually decide by our own deeds to allow them to take effect.

At this point we can turn to and consider in this light the karma exercise given by Rudolf Steiner on May 9, 1924. Practicing the exercise will perhaps lead us to a perception of the forces that shape destiny and help explain what occurs in a meeting.

Let me describe the exercise briefly. It takes three days to carry out. On the first day, you must recall as intensely as possible a situation you experienced a short time ago. You must "paint" the image of this experience in your soul as livingly as possible and in every detail. You see the person you have met, his or her physical aspect, gestures, behavior, as well as the environment where the meeting took place —all this with the greatest possible intensity. This is how the exercise begins, and it should be done with great care, for it sets in motion a stream of forces that will evolve over the next three days.

In the course of the three days and nights, the image is worked on by the different members or "envelopes" of the person practicing the exercise, undergoing a veritable transformation on its journey from the astral body to the ether body to the physical body. When you wake up after the third night, that is, on the morning of the fourth day, if the exercise has been successful, you will perceive a new image revealing the karmic context of the situation you pictured in your original image. At this point you see a scene from a past life where an event occurred that "provoked" the meeting in your present incarnation — the meeting preserved with an effort of memory at the beginning of the exercise.

Rudolf Steiner summarizes this process as follows:

1. Day One, Night One — Outside of the sleeping physical and ether bodies, the astral body works formatively on the image of the lived experience. The external ether impregnates the image with its own substance.

2. Day Two, Night Two — The image is impressed on the person's ether body by the astral body. During the

following night the ether body works on and elaborates the image.

3. Day Three, Night Three — The image is impressed on the person's physical body by the ether body. During the following night, the physical body works on and elaborates the image.

4. The morning of the fourth day — This image, totally transformed by now into an image of a past life, the "cause" of the scene represented on the first night, is the one you wake with."[15]

Rudolf Steiner comments that this exercise can help one recognize karmic relationships more quickly. However, all things being equal, a very strong will is required to carry it out. He emphasizes that this exercise must be done, not just 10 or 20 times, but 50 to 70 times before one can count on results. The process of the transformation of the image breaks down again and again. A power emanating from Ahriman, a being who does not want people to realize the possibility of looking into karma, repeatedly provokes this breakdown. Thus Rudolf Steiner speaks of the courage required to continue this exercise as long as is necessary.

The battles on this most important field of life, the struggles against the forces opposing human progress — opposing the knowledge and the practice of karma — raise the question of whether and where aid and protection are to be found. After the Christmas Conference of 1923, in the course of which he laid the Foundation Stone of the General Anthroposophical Society, that fundamental meditation, in the hearts of the members, Rudolf Steiner took up the question of karmic connections and of karma in general in an entirely new way. From that moment on, he explained, it was possible for him to speak freely of this eminently esoteric subject. As Ita Wegman puts it in her book *An die Freunde,* "The laws of karma were revealed. Before the Christmas Conference, it had not been possible to speak in such detail about karma and the laws governing it. . . . Revealing the mysteries of karma always calls up the greatest possible opposition from the Ahrimanic powers who want karma to remain veiled in mystery. This resistance had to be overcome if the Anthroposophical Society was not to be cut off from the youthful forces, the impulses of Michael." [16]

We are left to dwell on the question how is it possible to overcome the Ahrimanic forces. During the Christmas Conference of 1923, Rudolf Steiner entrusted the Anthroposophical Society's members with a meditation, the Foundation Stone,[17] planting it like a seed in the hearts of those present and those who have taken it up since then. The circle of radiance surrounding this seed — its influence — protects spiritual work as, for example, research in the field of karma. Again, Ita Wegman: "When karma is understood by means of heart and head forces, when repeated earth lives are looked at and understood without undue emotion or frivolity but in full earnestness, then it will be possible to overcome even the last anti-Michaelic demons, and the Age of Michael will find its continuation in the coming Christ-event." [18]

With all due caution, let us now look at the Foundation Stone in relation to Steiner's karma exercise of May 9, 1924. The Foundation Stone meditation consists of four parts. The first three parts address the human soul, asking it to carry out particular exercises. In the first part, we are asked to practice "spirit remembering," going all the way to the point of perceiving this memory. This activity of remembering ascends to the recognition of humanity's divine origin. After this exercise, students on this path "know that the supersensible was there first, with everything sense-perceptible developing out of it. They know that they themselves belonged to a supersensible world before they entered this sensory world for the first time." [19] Correspondingly, the first thing we do in the karma exercise of May 9, 1924, is to remember a personal karmic situation and picture it inwardly in an image, which then forms the point of departure for the exercise. Here too then we have the activity of remembering.

In the second part of the Foundation Stone, the exercise called for is to "practice spirit-mindfulness" — concentration of the spirit. Doesn't this mean that in the course of this meditation we must try to allow the spirit to penetrate ever deeper within us and that in this way our "feeling will be true"? In the karma exercise the second day is characterized by the fact that the image of the memory is impressed on the etheric body by the astral body, the seat of feeling.

Finally, the third exercise of the Foundation Stone brings us to the point of beholding: the soul must "practice spirit-beholding" — spirit vision. The soul is led to contemplate something — something spiritual.

What precisely do we contemplate thanks to the Foundation Stone meditation after this third exercise? It is said that our will becomes free; that our thinking becomes true. What do we perceive with these forces? We must take the next step and examine the fourth part of the Foundation Stone meditation.

In the first three parts the meditator recalls the spiritual history of human evolution, including the Fall from grace and the being bound to matter, while the fourth part spreads before his or her spiritual gaze the incarnation of the solar forces at the turning point of time. He or she becomes aware that "The spiritual light of the world has entered the stream of earthly existence." The deed of Christ becomes an experience for the mediator. Uniting Himself with a human body, the Christ canceled out, balanced the Fall from grace. He took upon himself the karma of humanity. He bore the sins of the world. On the fourth day of the karma exercises, corresponding to the fourth part of the Foundation Stone, the person practicing them sees in an image the karmic relation that provoked the original event. That morning, on awakening, one sees an image that "explains" the memory that was formed on the first evening.

Through meditative work with the Foundation Stone, we attain an exact vision of the cosmic karma of humanity's evolution in which the descent into matter (the Fall) is compensated for by the sacrifice of the solar being of Christ — the Light of the World. Thus there opens before us through this inner work an immense path that we can travel on a small scale in relation to our own personal karma with the karma exercise described above. Revealing the intimate relationship of Christ Jesus to the karma of the human being, the radiant aura of the Foundation Stone supports and protects the work we need to do in order to penetrate personal karma; it provides a spiritual basis for objectifying this work and placing it in the greater context of humanity's evolution.

This third stage of encounter, then, the stage of transformation or transubstantiation, is the moment of truth. A meeting, a human connection, becomes something else. It receives a new dimension. In order to work through this stage, we must truly transform ourselves so as to achieve a true relationship with another human being.

If we do not succeed, if we stop short at one of the preceding stages, no further progress is possible, and the crises which follow bring about not metamorphoses but repeated misunderstandings, painful struggles, and insoluble problems between the people in question. To conceal this tragedy of evolution, this failure to become aware of the profundity of an encounter, we cover up our inability with words like "That's life" or "That's karma," phrases — unfortunately all too common — in which an undertone of negative fatalism and resignation may be heard. If, on the other hand, we accept our own freedom, if we recognize the immense, sacred task of liberating religion, of sanctifying human encounters and feeling responsible for the course of a relationship, then this decision will give us courage and strength, and our meetings with others will become divine service, for "every meeting of person with person will be from the beginning a religious act, a sacrament." [20]

Appendix to Chapter IV

The Foundation Stone

In order to aid the reader in following the presentation, in the preceding section, of the correlation of the karma exercise and the Foundation Stone meditation, the Foundation Stone Mediation is appended here. Thus we can follow the path of the three exercises,

> Remembrance of the spirit,
> Concentration of the spirit,
> Contemplation of the spirit,

exercises which, when practiced in the sense that has been indicated, lead to the "seeing" of the fourth part:

> At the turning point of time
> the spiritual light of the worlds
> entered into the current of earthly becoming.

We may consider this fundamental meditation, the Foundation Stone, as an exercise leading to the contemplation of the Mystery of the Birth and Death of Christ Jesus. Let us therefore call it an exercise for research into "macrocosmic" karma. The exercise leading to the perception of individual karma can then be understood as being for research into "microcosmic" karma.

The translation that follows is based on the version of the Foundation Stone as Rudolf Steiner pronounced it on January 1, 1924, at the conclusion of the Christmas Conference. It differs a little from the official version published soon afterward. We have chosen it following its publication by Ernst Lehrs in his autobiography. Explaining this "expanded" version, Lehrs writes: "I have been able to give these additional passages thanks to the stenographic notes that Lili

Kolisko took for herself and her closest friends. I do so knowing the confidence that Rudolf Steiner placed in her consciousness and precision. . . . This version corresponds to the one which my friends and I often heard."[21]

Human soul!
You live in the limbs
that bear you through the world of space
into the essence of the ocean of the spirit.
Practice remembrance of the spirit
in depths of soul,
where, in the ruling
creator being of worlds,
your own I germinates
in the divine I.
Then you will live truly
in the human cosmic essence.

For the Father-Spirit of the heights rules
engendering being in the depths.
Seraphim, Cherubim, Thrones,
let resound in the heights
what echoes in the depths.
And what, in the echo of the depths,
lets the secret of the heights resound,
speaks:
Ex Deo nascimur.

The spirits of the elements hear it
in the east, the west, the north, the south.
May human beings also hear it!

Human soul!
You live in the beat of heart and lung
which leads you through the rhythm of time
into the essential feeling of your soul.
Practice concentration of the spirit
in balance of soul
where the wave of the deeds of cosmic becoming
unites your own I
with the I of the universe,
then your feeling will be true
in the acting of the human soul.

For in the space around rules
the will of Christ,
pouring his grace on souls
in the rhythms of the universe.
Through the Kyriotetes, Dynameis, Exousiai,
let there be set on fire, O spirits, by the east
what is formed by the west.
And the fire of the east,
that receives its form from the west,
speaks:
In Christo morimur.

The spirits of the elements hear it
in the east, the west, the north, the south.
May human beings also hear it!

Human soul!
You live in the peaceful head
which, for eternal reasons,
gives you access to cosmic thoughts;
practice contemplation of the spirit
in the peace of thoughts
where the eternal intentions of the gods
on your own I
to make your willing free
pour out in offering
the essential light of worlds.
Then you will think truly
in the depths of the human spirit

For the cosmic thoughts of the spirit rule,
imploring in the essence of the universe, light.
Principalities, Archangels, Angels
let prayer rise from the depths
that the heights may hear.
And when there will be correct understanding of
what sounds forth from the Principalities, Archangels,
Angels,
when what can be heard in the heights
will be prayed for from the depths,
then through the universe will resound the word:
Per Spiritum Sanctum Reviviscimus.

The spirits of the elements hear it
in the east, the west, the north, the south.
May human beings also hear it.

At the turning of the ages
the spiritual light of the worlds
entered the current of earthly becoming.
The dark night
concluded its rule.
The clear light of day
radiated in human hearts.

Light
which warms
the hearts of poor shepherds;
light
which illumines
the heads of wise Kings.

Light divine,
Christ-Sun,
warm our hearts,
illumine our heads,
that, founded in the forces of the heart,
dictated by the clear thought of the goal,
what we will
will be good.

V

Fragmentation and Unity

Fourth Stage: Communion

Only through religion do people become one.

Novalis

The requirements of evolution meant that humanity had to lose its unity in favor of the development of personality, but the impulse towards personality left humanity atomized, fragmented. The original language common to all human beings was lost, and humanity was split up into different peoples. This most important event has come down to us as an image in mythological consciousness: the story of the Tower of Babel.[22] After this event, the more humanity has progressed, the more evolutionary conditions forced individual human beings to confront themselves. In this way real spiritual progress set each human being the task of developing his or her own powers. Therefore isolation increases, accompanied by a feeling of solitude. At the same time, however, we must now take up and evolve a direction counter to this development. Since the fifteenth century, the development of the consciousness-soul — stimulated by scientific consciousness and technological achievements — has brought humanity to a point which allows individual personalities to unfold completely, but isolates them as a result. To forge a path to a new unity now seems a vital necessity, but there are two conditions attached to this way:

1. People must actively choose this way: the will must be involved (this is a corollary of freedom).
2. The way must be clearly defined.

The goal of the new unity is called Communion.

In the fourth part of the Mass — the Communion — bread and wine are shared out. Members of the congregation wishing to do so come to the invisible table and are unified through this common repast. Through the priest's Offering and through the Transubstantiation, bread and wine have become the body and blood of Christ. The bread, the Holy Host, has the shape of a little sun, and the sun forces taken up through it serve to unify the members of the congregation. There is a mystery here, however, with regard to the solar forces of the Christ — they work on a general human level and yet have access to single individualities.

The Christic solar forces have, in fact, a double quality: they are objectively universal, and yet they support the development of free individuality. As Rudolf Steiner writes:

> We do not owe our individuality to the sun. The sun shines on the good and the evil, on men of genius and on fools. As far as earthly life is concerned the sun has no direct connection with our individuality. In one instance only has the sun established connection with earthly individuality and this was possible because at a certain point in the earth's evolution, a sublime sun being, the Christ, did not remain on the sun but came down from the sun to the earth and became a being of the earth in the body of a man, thus uniting his own cosmic destiny with the destiny of earthly humanity. Thus, through becoming an earthly being, the Sun-being of Christ gained access to single human individualities.[23]

The solar beings who remain on the sun lack this particularity of the Christ; they have only general access to humanity as a whole. However, Christ did retain one attribute of sun-beings which can be a source of great blessing for the human race, namely, that His activity does not discriminate among human beings:

What remained in Him was and is that his power knows no differentiation among human beings. Christ is not the Christ of this or that nation, of this or that rank or class. He is the Christ for all human beings, without distinction of class, race or nation. Nor is He the Christ of particular individualities, inasmuch as his help is available alike to the genius and the fool. The Christ impulse has access to the individuality of human beings, but to become effective it must take effect in the inmost depths of human nature. It is not the forces of the intellect but the deepest forces of the heart and soul which can receive the Christ impulse; but once received this impulse works not for the benefit of the individual-human but of the universal-human. This is because Christ is a solar being.[24]

The powers of Christ can solve the following problem connected to the existential situation of human beings in their relation to each other: how can I fully develop my individuality in a community of individuals? Transposed to the field of human encounters, this question reads, "How can I intimately relate my individuality to that of another human being without losing it?" The first three stages of an encounter, as we have described them above, constitute a first attempt at an answer: Mutual recognition on the physical plane, proceeding through sacrifice and the recognition and understanding of a common destiny, can provide a new basis for meeting forged from the spirit.

A new community forms thanks to a spiritual impulse. What really unites people shows itself clearly: the spirit that brings us together reveals itself. We commune in Christ, the Lord of destiny. He wants people to rediscover each other so that what is universally human can prevail anew among them. It was for this that He came down among us.

This is the final stage of encounter. After a process that can last hours, days, and even years, those who have met each other are permitted to experience the forces of communion. Grace descends upon them, and they sense the flames of the Holy Spirit forging them into a new unity.

This fourth stage, Communion, may also therefore be called a Pentecostal event. The process of the encounter passes through several metamorphoses, so to speak, and then ends with the mystery of what occurred at Whitsun or Pentecost: the participants in the encounter form a new unity, but without losing their essential individuality.

How should we understand Pentecost in the light of the new — Michaelic — mysteries? Again, some of Rudolf Steiner's thoughts can provide enlightenment. What he has to say in the lecture cycle *The Easter Festival in the Evolution of the Mysteries* about the real significance of the seasons or festivals of the year is quite foreign, even shocking, to the way we look at things today.[25] Of Easter, for instance, he says the following:

> For Christians Easter commemorates the Resurrection. The corresponding pagan festival taking place at approximately the same time of year as Easter in a sense celebrated the resurrection of nature, the reawakening of what, as nature, had been asleep throughout the winter. However, the similarity ends there. It must be emphasized that with regard to its inner meaning, the Christian Easter festival in no way corresponds to the pagan equinox celebrations. Rather, a serious examination of ancient pagan times reveals that Easter, in the Christian sense, is related to the festivals that grew out of the mysteries that were celebrated in the fall.
>
> This most curious fact demonstrates what serious misunderstandings regarding matters of the highest importance have occurred in the course of humanity's development. In the early Christian centuries, nothing less happened than the confusion of Easter with a completely different festival, with the result that Easter was moved from fall to spring.

The ancient festival Rudolf Steiner speaks of here is the festival of Adonis or Attys. Adonis represents "all that manifests itself in human beings as vigorous youth and beauty. . . . Many indeed took the image of Adonis to be the actually present god, the god of beauty and youthful strength, of an unfolding seminal power that reveals in splendorous outer existence all the inner nobility and grandeur of which humanity is capable." In autumn, in the course of religious festivities, the image of this god was plunged in the sea, then brought up out of the water after three days. Then "the laments gave way to songs of joy and hymns to the resurrected god, the god who had come back to life."

This ritual took place in autumn, when the earth loses its mantle of plants and leaves, at the moment when nature is dying. In the lectures quoted here, Rudolf Steiner explains how the understanding of resurrection can be found and expanded at that time of year, autumn, when the forces of nature offer no support. "Humanity was to contemplate the dying of nature in order to recognize that human beings die as well, but that in accordance with their inner nature they arise anew in the spiritual world. The purpose of these ancient pagan Mystery festivals was thus to reveal the true meaning of death." [26]

The Mystery festivals taking place in the spring on the other hand confronted people with the beginning of life, the mysteries of birth and of the descent into matter. Candidates for initiation into these spring mysteries were also led into the mystery of how the forces of nature experience resurrection at this time of year. This is in stark contrast to the autumn mysteries, as Rudolf Steiner shows: "If we look back in time, we see that human beings' descent from pre-earthly to earthly existence was recognized in certain mysteries, while other mysteries, the autumn mysteries, recognized their ascent to the spiritual." [27]

The Mystery of Golgotha took place in spring. Rudolf Steiner indicated April 3 as the date of Christ's death on the cross. In The Calendar of the Soul, published in 1912, we find him writing: "April 3, 33 A.D., is the date of the Mystery of Golgotha, according to spiritual-scientific investigations." [28] What candidates for initiation in the spring Mysteries were allowed to experience — in advance as it were — this actually became reality through Christ's deed. Again, as Rudolf Steiner has indicated, a historical misunderstanding resulted in Easter being confused with a completely different festival. The reason was that human beings were no longer capable of experiencing resurrection in the autumn; to understand resurrection they needed the support of the burgeoning nature forces of spring. Summing up his lecture of April 21, 1924, Steiner says that for human beings, but not for nature, the true festival of Easter is clearly related to autumn. For nature, Easter occurs in spring when the spirit causes the natural world to sprout and spring forth out of the earth:

> Resurrection of the human being: autumn
> Resurrection of nature: spring.

For human beings, Easter is an autumn mystery. "At the time when nature declines and dies away, human beings should think about their ascent, their inward elevation, their resurrection in the spirit." [29] Novalis, for whom this mystery was transparent, wrote in one of his fragments: "When a spirit dies, it becomes a human being; a human being who dies becomes a spirit. A free death of the spirit, a free death of the human being."

Since the beginning of the new Age of Michael in the last third of the nineteenth century (1879, according to anthroposophical research), it has become possible, even necessary, thanks to anthroposophy, to distinguish between these two Easter festivals, at first theoretically and then as a matter of experience. The festival of Easter, bound up with the mysteries of spring and the resurrection of nature, that is, of physical and etheric forces, is followed by the Feast of Pentecost, celebrated seven weeks later. But what is there in the Easter Festival that is connected with the autumn mystery? Is there a connection ? And if so, where to find it, how to understand it?

The experience we have in the fall when we perceive the forces of death taking hold of nature and we penetrate these forces of death consciously — this experience leads us to a more profound understanding of the forces of resurrection. We awaken to the spirit. Such would be the experience of Pentecost in relation with the mystery of autumn: to awaken to the spirit, to the individual spirit reborn in every soul. At what moment of the year can this happen in the new Mysteries? Undoubtedly, at Christmas.

Rudolf Steiner often spoke of the need for a new understanding of Christmas. For instance, in his lecture cycle *The Spiritual Communion of Humanity* he said:

> Eventually the human race will not be content with simply looking back over biblical accounts of Christ Jesus' spiritual journeying on earth, but will understand that since that time, Christ has united with human beings in earthly life and still reveals Himself to them, if they only listen. In our own time, humanity will be able to come to the insight that, just as the festival of Christmas follows Michaelmas in the cycle of the year, the new revelation of Michael which began one autumn in the last third of the nineteenth century will need to be followed by a festival of consecration, a Christmas, which will enable us to acquire an understanding of spiritual birth, of the birth in the spirit humanity needs in order to continue on its earthly journey so that the earth can be spiritualized and transformed in the future. It is not simply that we are now in the autumn of the year and that the annual Christmas is coming. We are living in a time when we should comprehend the Michael-revelation which began in the last third of the nineteenth century, comprehend it in the very depths of our souls and out of our own human nature, and when we should also be looking for a way towards a true Christmas festival, a festival of the indwelling of the spirit we strive to recognize.[30]

To understand this passage correctly is to realize that a new Christmas festival needs to accompany any new Michael festival in the fall. The festival of Easter in the spring, as festival of resurrection, and the event of Pentecost some weeks later, provide forces that save the physical and etheric aspects of the natural world, and thereby also human beings, insofar as they are natural creatures, from death. Christ's deed on Golgotha and his Resurrection at Easter have made it possible for nature and humanity to continue to live. Thus the danger has been avoided of a physical and etheric hardening that have made it impossible for human souls to find bodies on earth into which to incarnate.

But ever since humanity received the consciousness-soul, each individual human being must personally want to undergo death and resurrection in relationship to Michael. The possibility of doing so is open to all human beings every autumn, the Michaelic moment of the year. The Michaelic impulse of autumn, a force of resurrection, can surmount a second, new danger — the danger of the human soul shutting itself off more and more within itself until it no longer provides a dwelling place for the spirit. Christ Jesus rose living from the grave: this is Easter in spring. Living individual human beings must descend of their own free choice into the grave: this is Easter in autumn. Such individuals will have a conscious experience of the forces of resurrection and for them Christmas becomes a new Pentecost: a festival of the birth of spiritual individuality in the soul. "The time has come when we need to find a way from Michaelmas to a mid-winter celebration which includes a sunrise of the spirit." [31]

These considerations point to an essential aspect of the Christmas Conference of 1923. Laying the Foundation Stone, the fundamental meditation that unites the new community, laying it in the depths of the human heart, Rudolf Steiner "baptized humanity anew" [32] with the fire of the Holy Spirit. In the course of this celebration of a new humanity, each participant was able to experience the birth of individuality, linked by virtue of the Foundation Stone with other individualities, and so a community was born where the flame of the Holy Spirit united human beings in a common task. From this point of view, the Christmas Conference can be seen as a Pentecost event — Christmas understood in the sense of the new Michaelic mysteries: Christmas as a spiritual birth. This is the new communion in which human beings feel connected through the spirit. Now roots must be sought in the spirit, no longer in the blood. No longer blood brothers and sisters, we are brothers and sisters in the spirit. The spiritual bond is now as strong as was the blood-bond. And surely what Rudolf Steiner said in conclusion to those gathered for the laying of the Foundation Stone on December 25, 1923, sounds like the message of Pentecost:

> And if you hear this resounding in your own hearts, my dear friends, then what you will establish here will be a true union of human beings on behalf of Anthroposophia, and will carry the spirit which prevails in radiant thought-light around our dodecahedral stone of love out into the world, where it may shed light and warmth on the progress of human souls and the progress of the world.[33]

The thoughts on communion — the fourth stage of the process of encounter — developed here in relation to the Christmas Conference, that is, to the new mysteries, indicate the special quality of this communion. We can consider the Christmas Conference as a meeting of, an encounter between, 800 people brought together by their destiny for a common act. On several occasions during the Christmas Conference, Rudolf Steiner insisted that the participants' deed was what mattered — that an action accomplished by the participants themselves was required.

What came to pass in this December 1923, on the level of humanity as such in relationship to the cosmos, is a seed for communion as the fourth stage in any meeting of two or more people. The process of human encounter leads to communion, to the participants' finding a new relationship to each other, a new bond, whose roots are purely spiritual. Lunar forces lead us toward each other. The process of encounter completed, solar forces radiate between us. A community founded in the spirit has been born.[34]

VI

Transformation of Consciousness During an Encounter

Mary Magdalene Meets the Risen Christ

How do we see physically? No differently than we do in our consciousness — by means of the productive power of imagination. Consciousness is the eye and ear, the sense for inner and outer meaning.

Novalis

Our consideration of encounters has shown us that what happens during the process of meeting another person is linked to a transformation of consciousness. As the archetype of the human forces that lead people toward each other, we chose the meeting of John and Jesus at the Baptism in the Jordan. Another archetype exemplifies the process of transformation of consciousness during an encounter: the meeting of Mary Magdalene with the Risen Christ, as recounted in the twentieth chapter of St. John's Gospel.

Mary comes to the tomb on Easter morning and discovers the absence of Jesus' body. The body that she loved so dearly on a human level has disappeared: it is not there. We have already shown how, in the course of the first stage of an encounter, the physical body of the other as perceived by the senses must be met with great interest and love. The physical appearance of another human being, when it is perceived with sufficient interest, sets the whole process in motion. We wake up to the other. We may say then, without fear of being wrong, that Mary Magdalene had awakened fully to the external, physical aspect of Christ Jesus. But in order to go any further, in order to move to the second stage, it is

53

necessary to look for the other person's true image. A person's outer appearance, the point of departure for the entire process, despite its importance, is after all merely Maya, an illusion: it must be overcome, it must disappear, yielding its place to something higher.

Here, the physical having disappeared, Mary Magdalene awakens to another stage of consciousness by "turning around." This transformation of consciousness enables her to see the etheric. She sees the true image of Christ Jesus: the "gardener" who now wants to cultivate the earth, to tend it so as to receive its true fruits. That is, she finds herself in full consciousness before the etheric Christ. But she has not consciously grasped the real relationship between them. Her consciousness must be raised again in order for her to understand Him. Christ Himself prompts her, aids her in attaining the necessary degree of consciousness. He calls her name, "Mary." Then her consciousness is raised, as signified by these words — "and she turned around again."

Obviously, this "turning around" is not meant to be taken literally for she turns around twice, which is absurd from a physical point of view. Rather, what is meant is that different forces of cognition, different states of consciousness are in question — first imagination, then inspiration. Thus this encounter becomes gradually clearer by a process of cognition. The karmic relationship to the Risen One becomes conscious. "Rabbi, Master!" she says. This is the third stage: she recognizes him fully.

The final stage, Communion, total union one with the other, is not yet possible at this point in evolution: "Do not touch me!" says the Risen One.

Appendix to Chapter VI

Gospel of St. John, XX: 11–17
(King James Version)

11 But Mary stood without at the sepulcher weeping: and as she wept, she stooped down, and looked into the sepulcher, 12and seeth two angels in white sitting, the one at the head, and the other at the feet, where the body of Jesus had lain. 13 And they say unto her, Woman, why weepest thou? She saith unto them, Because they have taken away my Lord, and I know not where they have laid him. 14 And when she had thus said, she *turned herself back*, and saw Jesus standing, and *knew* not that it was Jesus. 15 Jesus saith unto her, Woman, why weepest thou? She, supposing him to be the gardener, saith unto him, Sir, if thou have borne him hence, tell me where thou hast laid him, and I will take him away. 16 Jesus saith unto her, Mary. She *turned herself*, and saith unto him, Rabboni; which is to say, Master. 17 Jesus saith unto her, Touch me not; for I am not yet ascended to my Father: but go to my brethren, and say unto them, I ascend unto my Father, and your Father; and to my God, and your God. [Emphasis added]

VII

Human Beings and their Relationship
to the Gods who Shape Destiny

*In any case this world is the result of an interplay between
myself and the divinity. Everything that exists, everything
that comes about, comes from being touched by the spirit.*

Novalis

Rudolf Steiner has drawn our attention to two important points concerning anthroposophy:

1. anthroposophy must fructify life;
2. Europeans must seek the spirit through the senses, through sense perceptions.

In *The Work of the Angels in Man's Astral Body*, for example, Steiner says: "The anthroposophical grasp of the spirit should not be merely theoretical philosophy. It should be the constant content and vital force in our daily lives. Only when we are in a position to empower the anthroposophical grasp of the spirit, so that it really becomes fully alive in us, only then will it actually fulfill its task." [35] And in *The Mission of Folk Souls*, Steiner states that: "The European race in particular, with its strong sensory orientation, must apply itself to the task of finding a way to the spirit through the senses." [36]

Is there an example in which the anthroposophical grasp of the spirit can become a content of life, a vital force? Is this not the case when we seek to permeate our daily lives with some religious substance? Certainly; and the foundation, the basis of any permeation of daily life with religious substance, is to strive to know as an experience that "through flesh and blood something appears in each human being

57

that reveals itself as coming from divine cosmic depths." [37] The angels pursue a goal, that of weaving into human souls this ideal: "In the future each human being will see hidden in his neighbor a divine being." Such words give us an idea of what could come into play between people when they try to live their encounters as religious acts, as "acts of consecration."

To put it differently, an activity we perform in everyday life becomes religious if it establishes our connection to the gods. Remember what we said at the beginning: that human encounters are the affair not of humans alone but also of the gods. In a lecture given soon after the Christmas Conference, Steiner expressed some thoughts concerning human encounters considered from the point of view of anthroposophical knowledge. If we wanted to give a title to this passage we could call it: *On the Importance of Human Encounters for the Gods.*

> The gods have already lived through what happens to us when we meet another person. They went through this experience in advance as a consequence of what we did with the person in question in a previous earthly life. . . . Thus the activity of these divine beings of the first hierarchy, of the seraphim, cherubim and thrones, was determined by their human creatures on earth. And then, in turn, they experienced in advance the destiny they were preparing for us for a lifetime still to come.[38]

Consequently we must realize that *the forces arising during an encounter derive from a divine substance.* The gods have lived *this*, and we can come into relation with the gods if we are able to seize *this* consciously and render it transparent. The situation is depicted in the accompanying diagram.

Our path toward the divine in the other human being, in humanity, begins through the senses. (This is the first stage of the encounter.) Our task then becomes to return this divine element to the gods. This is the "reverse ritual." [39] It is the stage that follows the encounter. Finally, after death, in recapitulating our life, we re-experience the encounter in

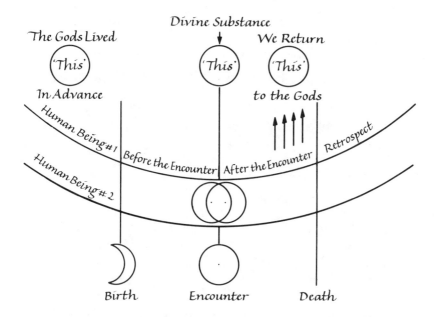

the spiritual world, but much more consciously. In communion with the gods, and in the full light of consciousness, we
prepare the divine element for our next incarnation. In our
next life, we will encounter the other person again, but under
the star of the new Mysteries, that is, knowing what we
decided between death and rebirth. We shall then understand the meaning of this encounter. Although this understanding may seem an ideal distant from our present lifetime,
we must nevertheless strive for it consciously so that in
subsequent incarnations we will be able to experience human
encounters as "free religious acts." [40]

Rudolf Steiner was in full possession of this awareness, as
the following description by Zeylmans van Emmichoven
reveals.

I went to Dornach in December, 1920. My relationship
to anthroposophy had grown to the point where I had
a strong desire to meet Rudolf Steiner, and it was indeed

a decisive experience. The details were as follows: On
the evening of December 17, I was sitting in the lecture
hall with my fiancee, who was studying eurythmy in
Dornach. We were waiting for Rudolf Steiner's lecture
to begin. It was bitterly cold outside, and Dornach was
covered with snow. All of a sudden the blue curtain at
one side of the stage opened and Rudolf Steiner, whom
I recognized from photographs, walked up to the lec-
tern. At that moment I had an undeniable experience
of recognizing someone I had known before, to the
point where a whole series of pictures hinting at earlier
situations appeared before me as if I were looking at a
man who had been my teacher down through the mil-
lennia.[41]

After the lecture, Zeylmans von Emmichoven was introduced to Rudolf Steiner, who said to him, "I've been expect-
ing you here for a long time." Zeylmans took this to imply
that he had already been in Dornach for some time and
therefore replied, "But sir, I only arrived late this afternoon!"
Rudolf Steiner smiled happily and said, "I didn't mean it
that way at all."[42]

Thus, for an initiate, an encounter is completely transparent. And for us? Is not the substance that we can perceive
arising during an encounter a divine substance? Yes, it is a
divine substance, since human beings are the thoughts of the
gods.[43]

The gods think, and human beings arise. True communion occurs when we perceive a human being as a divine
thought in the reality of karma.

Epilogue

Over the years significant steps have been taken in many areas to rise to Rudolf Steiner's challenge to fructify our daily life by means of anthroposophy — for instance, in education, agriculture, medicine and many different artistic, social and economic fields. In this context the reality of human encounters occupies a central place. Human encounters are moments in the evolution of the world. They affect individual human acts in relation to other human beings —the teacher meets the students, the doctor meets the patients — in such a way that consciousness of what happens during these meetings becomes ever more important.

There are still two questions of general interest to be discussed. The first one is whether each of the four stages —

Proclamation,
Sacrifice (Offertory),
Transubstantiation,
Communion

— must be brought to a conclusion before one can move to the next stage. Obviously, each stage needs to be brought to some kind of ripeness before we can proceed to the next. However, in reality, the stages overlap. The attending to the physical elements of the other (Proclamation) can go on for a long time before it is experienced fully. It is important that our interest in the external aspect of the other person not diminish, that our interest be constantly renewed. We must not stop after acquiring some knowledge, as if it were final. Likewise, the sacrifice of our own personality (Offertory) is something that must happen repeatedly, and for the sake of progress, our willingness to make this offering must never fade, we must never stop practicing active tolerance. When we are in search of transformation and the perception of real karmic relationships (Transubstantiation), patience, suffering, and constancy are the prerequisites of progress. And

61

finally, Communion allows humility and gratitude to be born in the soul. Thus each stage is sustained by its own moral qualities, and there are different levels to be passed through at each stage.

The second question is whether all participants in a human encounter must progress at the same pace. We need to know whether the two people in question are both unfamiliar with anthroposophy, whether one is an anthroposophist while the other knows nothing about it, or whether they are both anthroposophists. In the first instance, both people can go through the process quite involuntarily. This corresponds to what Rudolf Steiner called "initiation through life." In the second instance, it is natural that the person who has some knowledge of anthroposophy should feel responsible for the situation and its development. For anthroposophy helps one to understand and aid the other. In the last instance, both persons are responsible. If one happens to notice that the other does not follow what is happening, that one should endure this delay patiently and, without interrupting his or her own development, try to advance the process, always making an effort to accompany the other person attentively.

A striking example of this situation is given by the incident between Rudolf Steiner and Zeylmans van Emmichoven related at the end of the last chapter. Rudolf Steiner was in possession of a consciousness which permitted him an overview of all karmic relationships. With infinite patience he tried, through lectures, meditations and exercises, to widen the awareness of members of the Anthroposophical Society — and of all in the twentieth century — to the point where Communion can be consciously experienced. The Christmas Conference is a seed for this. What Rudolf Steiner experienced at the level of humanity is valid for all of us in our own domains.

Of course, many questions remain to be answered. The ideas developed here are meant to serve as a stimulus for deepening this important theme of human encounters. But this deepening can also be attained by practicing what has been described — in the sense that Novalis means when he says, "We know only to the extent that we do."

PART TWO

ENCOUNTERING
A POET
THROUGH HIS
WORK

I

Preliminary Remarks

Meeting other human beings is a daily reality assuming the most diverse aspects and occurring in the most varied situations. In the first part of this book we studied encounters as they happen on earth between incarnated human beings who are led to meet each other by the forces of destiny.

There are other kinds of encounter, however, which put us into relation with human beings who have left the physical plane. Such beings leave traces here on earth, in our souls. In this category belong those geniuses, writers, and poets who have left us works to which our souls are drawn. Our souls nourish themselves on these works, developing by contact with the ideas and images created by their authors.

How does such a meeting with an author occur? I believe that the stages sketched out in the first part of this book maintain their vigor and relevance and can, in the measure that we pass through them consciously, lead us to the being who created such a work on earth.

Let us recapitulate the stages:

1. Interest in the outer aspect of the being encountered. Here, the study of the poet's work.

2. The sacrifice of personal thoughts, whereby we allow the ideas and images of the work we are studying to live in us. In the Manuscript of Barr, written by Rudolf Steiner for Edouard Schure, we read: "We only attain knowledge by renouncing our own absolute point of view and immersing ourselves in spiritual streams foreign to us." [44]

3. The study of the karmic relationships of the author under consideration. In Rudolf Steiner's works we find unveiled the karmic pasts of many authors.

4. Communion, through the work, with the author being studied.

Thus one can see that a range of encounters is possible, even if the partner in the encounter is an author who has left the terrestrial plane. The stages of the encounter remain, at bottom, the same.

Therefore we would like, starting with certain poems of Victor Hugo, and with the help of indications given by Rudolf Steiner in 1924 concerning the incarnations of our poet[45], to attempt the adventure of such a meeting.

From time to time in the cultural life of a people a personality will arise whose life and work marks with great intensity the people and the spiritual life of the epoch. The radiance of such a personality often overflows the limits of a single country to enrich the evolution of the universal human spirit. Consequently, we may be inspired to ask what deep impulses are at work in the soul of such a genius.

In his lectures entitled *Karmic Relationships*[46] Rudolf Steiner examined carefully and with intense interest the life and work of certain personalities of human spiritual, cultural and social life, in order to illustrate in a living way the evolution of these exceptional beings in the course of their different incarnations. In the book *Theosophy*[47] the ideas of reincarnation and karma are studied scientifically. We learn that the human entelechy, in its evolution, passes through successive earthly lives. That is to say, it is rooted in the development of the earth itself, in which it participates by means of its own evolution. The chapter on this theme in *Theosophy* remains, however, entirely in the realm of abstraction — the concepts, chiseled by a thinking schooled in scientific process, form a coherent and intelligible whole. As we read it, we follow a solid line of thinking, showing that reincarnation may be investigated scientifically as an idea.

It becomes clear that a human being may be understood on three levels. Insofar as we are bodily beings, we are immersed in the stream of heredity whereas, on a soul level, it is the laws of karma that guide our becoming. Lastly, the spiritual entity, the eternal kernel, can only be understood within the context of reincarnation, which is the progressive, evolutionary rhythm of our whole being.

In 1924, however, in *Karmic Relationships*, Rudolf Steiner adopts a completely different point of view. Presupposing a scientific study of the chapter on karma and reincarnation in *Theosophy*, he attempts with the aid of numerous examples to illustrate ideas relating to this theme.

Before 1924, Steiner had certainly described personalities in the evolutionary perspective of successive lives — those of Elijah, for example, as well as other individualities dealt with in *Occult History*.[48] Following the Christmas Conference of 1923, however, which was the occasion of the complete renewal of the Anthroposophical Society, he began to develop the theme in a systematic manner, multiplying examples that firmly supported the fundamental ideas of karma. Reading these lectures awakens in us the powerful feeling that Rudolf Steiner wanted to encourage a systematic study of the examples he gave, thereby leading us eventually toward our own personal research. The very concrete examples of biographies in relation to previous incarnations allow us on the one hand to conceptualize the laws of human development through several incarnations and on the other to uncover the method used by Steiner himself in his spiritual researches into karma. Furthermore, an exercise to aid these researches is explained in one of the lectures.[49]

Thus the impulse may be born in us to occupy ourselves with one or another of the personalities studied in his lectures. Indeed, it seems that in the work of such an individuality a reflection of his previous incarnations may be discovered. It was in this way that the author of these lines was profoundly moved by reading Steiner's revelations concerning Victor Hugo. Steiner presents Hugo as having been in one of his previous incarnations an initiate of the Hibernian or Irish Mysteries. Reading the description of these Mysteries in the lecture cycle entitled *Mystery Knowledge and Mystery Centres*[50] revealed such a coincidence with the content of some of Hugo's poems that it became evident that Hugo's experiences in his previous Irish incarnation transparently shone through these poems.

The poem "The Vision From Which This Book Emerged," from *The Legend of the Centuries*, is a dazzling example.[51] Indeed, in his spiritual researches on Hugo, Steiner observes that, following his incarnation as an Irish initiate, Hugo enlarged his experiences between death and a new birth, above all in the sphere of Saturn. The spiritual beings ruling on Saturn have a very distinct function: that of intensely living the past, of contemplating humanity's past with all their forces. The first part of this study dedicated to Victor Hugo will try to show that this poem very clearly reflects these experiences between death and a new birth.[52] The second part, by means of convergent examples, and in line with the same process, presents poems that clearly could only have been written and can only be understood against the background of the spiritual trials and victories of an initiation into the Hibernian Mysteries, such as Steiner describes them.

Thus by means of a meditative reading one can approach a human individuality and encounter him in a purely spiritual manner through his work.

II

Victor Hugo
and the Sphere of Saturn

Every human being is a god's
destiny walking on the earth.

Victor Hugo

May 18, 1885, Victor Hugo, eighty-three years old, was struck by a congestion of the brain. Four days later, on May 22, he died. In his death agony, he spoke these last lines of poetry: "Here is the battle of day against night"; and, in his final moments, his last words were: "I see black light."

While he lived Hugo was either loved or hated. He died in an apotheosis, led to his tomb by over a million French men and women. His voice dominated the century, and yet today he remains unknown to many. "No writer in France is more unknown than V. Hugo," wrote Mauriac.[53] People today are unfavorably disposed or even hostile to him. Therefore it is not unusual to read in a textbook that "the young no longer read Hugo." And yet the reading of his poetry, his powers of evocation cannot leave one indifferent. Where did he obtain this gift, this magic, what qualities of soul allow him to move so directly in these astonishing and evocative rhythms, these depths?

Of one of his own heroes, Hugo himself wrote: "He looks at nature so much that nature has disappeared," and that "nothing can resist the calm, deep steadiness of the eyes," since "nature is an appearance corrected by a transparency." [54] Baudelaire immediately understood his greatness. "When one imagines what French poetry was before he appeared, and what a renewal it has undergone since he has come; when one imagines what it would have been had he not come . . . it is impossible not to consider him as one of those rare, providential spirits who, in the order of literature, effect the salvation of us all." [55]

To better approach Hugo, to better understand this complex individual, let us adopt a completely different point of view. Let us examine his work in the light of anthroposophy or spiritual science. Rudolf Steiner expressed this point of view very clearly:

> We really only understand another human being when we consider him or her in relation to the evolution that has been undergone between death and a new birth. Studying another human being in this way we perceive the totality of his moral, religious, and ethical qualities. A person is not impoverished by this, but enriched by the fact that he is studied in the light of the spirit.[56]

To fully understand this quotation one must know that Rudolf Steiner by his powers of spiritual investigation followed souls after death on their light-filled cosmic journey. The theme of the karma lectures is dedicated to the experiences of the human soul after death, or more exactly to the life of the soul between death and a new birth. On its cosmic itinerary the soul, freed from the physical body and growing ever larger, first passes through the spheres of the Moon, Mercury, and Venus, and then through those of the Sun, Mars, Jupiter, and Saturn. Thereafter, the soul can unite itself with the stars and can participate in universal cosmic life, before concentrating herself once again, in a "descending" path, toward a new earthly incarnation. For the student of spiritual science these lives between death and a new birth furnish the bases for the understanding of the earthly incarnation. Studying certain individualities in his lectures on karmic relationships, particularly those of 1924, Steiner demonstrates the importance of such knowledge for understanding an individual such as Victor Hugo.

What, then, are the sidereal influences — after death or before birth — that particularly inspired the life of this poet?

According to Steiner:

The impulses of Saturn have a very special influence on the human being. Even the perception of them . . . even the sight of the Mysteries of Saturn is in many respects shattering; these Mysteries, in a sense, are alien to earthly life. And whoever gradually learns through initiation-knowledge to perceive the Mysteries of Saturn . . . undergoes experiences of dramatic intensity, shattering experiences, that are harder and harder to bear because these Mysteries strike at the very roots of life. Nevertheless it can be said that we become aware of the whole wonderful setting of a human being's life when we perceive how karma takes shape in this sphere.[57]

We may ask ourselves, Steiner adds, where one may find these initiates of the ancient Mysteries. What must be understood is that a person can have been initiated in full consciousness during an earthly life; but then upon a later return to earth the wisdom of this initiation may lie hidden in the depths of his or her soul. Present-day human bodies, as well as the education we undergo, have become major obstacles to the direct expression of the qualities of soul acquired in such a past initiation. Former initiates can therefore reappear in modern life, but now endowed with a greatness that is not directly spiritual — for example they may manifest as politicians, writers, scientists, businessmen, and so on.

I would like to give you an example [Steiner continues] of a personality who, in a former earthly life, was actually initiated into the Hibernian Mysteries, the Mysteries of ancient Ireland, during the first Christian century when those great Mysteries were already in decline, though still preserving far-reaching, profound knowledge. This personality was initiated to a high degree. Now the knowledge possessed by these Irish Mysteries was especially profound, not in an intellectual but in

an intensely human sense. . . . This Hibernian initiate
became Victor Hugo.

Baudelaire, who was a genius in his perception of the
intimate "correspondences" of things, expressed himself in
this way concerning Hugo: "Victor Hugo was, from the
beginning, the most gifted, the most visibly chosen to express
what I would call the mystery of life. . . . No artist is more
universal than he or more able to put himself into contact
with the forces of universal life . . . he saw the mystery
everywhere. Thus Hugo possessed not only greatness, but
universality." [58]

In "universality" is the "universe." Baudelaire's article should
be quoted in full. Every phrase confirms Steiner's words
that the depth of the Hibernian Mysteries was "especially
profound, not in an intellectual but in an intensely human
sense." This reminds us of Gide's celebrated remark. Asked
who was the greatest poet of the nineteenth century, Gide
replied, "Victor Hugo, alas!" [59]

Luckily others, besides the intelligent Gide, have seen
more clearly this universality, this humanity that Hugo de-
rived from his previous incarnation, as the two following
quotations show:

> Intelligence illuminates the clever man. But to predict
> what no one hopes for and nobody wants — that goes
> beyond intelligence. From that derives the glory of
> being jeered which, for our poet [Hugo], still occurs
> today. (Alain)[60]

> Yes, the Master of French Words, that was one of his
> titles. But there was another and more dazzling: the
> Master of Universal Feelings.[61]

These two quotations precisely illustrate — and all honor
is due to these two authors for seeing it, even if they did not
know clearly what they saw — what lived in Hugo's soul as
the reflection of his initiation. What lived there came, as we
have seen, from Mysteries of a quite special depth, not in

an intellectual, but in a purely human sense. In the continuation of the 1924 lecture,[62] from which we have already quoted, Steiner speaks of the Hibernian Initiate. (In the next chapter we shall discuss what he has to say.) Then he goes on to characterize the sequence of Hugo's incarnations:

> Now there is a personality upon whom the Initiation rites and ceremonies of the Hibernian Mysteries had made a profound impression; they had a deep effect on his inner life and his experiences were of such intensity that he forgot the earth altogether. Then, after this personality had lived through an incarnation as a woman, when the impulses of the earlier Initiation showed themselves merely in the general disposition of the soul, he came to earth again as an important figure in the 19th century. . . .

Here Steiner describes an important aspect of the life of the poet between death and a new birth. Whereas Voltaire, of whom he speaks in the same lecture, had undergone two influences: that of Arab culture in a past incarnation and, between death and a new birth, that of the Sphere of Mars, Hugo, by contrast, before being reborn and appearing in the personality of the poet of the nineteenth century, had undergone quite other experiences. It is the understanding of these experiences that will illuminate in a startling manner one of his poems. Steiner writes:

> [Hugo] had lived out the consequences of his karma in the sphere of Saturn — the sphere where one lives among Beings who, fundamentally speaking, have no present. It is a shattering experience to look with clairvoyant vision into the sphere of Saturn, where Beings live who have no present but only look back on their past.

Then come the essential phrases which allow us to enter so deeply into one of Hugo's most beautiful, enigmatic poems — one that we cannot truly understand, whose veil we cannot pierce, unless we know the hidden impulses that were at work in the poet's soul.

This personality of whom I am speaking, who had at one time been initiated and had thus, in a certain sense, transcended earthly existence, bore his soul to those Beings who take no part in the present, and elaborated his karma among them. It was as if everything that had been experienced hitherto in an Initiate-existence now illumined with majestic splendor all the past earthly lives. This past was brought to fruition by what had been experienced through the Hibernian Initiation.

The poem in question is the one which opens the epic collection *The Legend of the Centuries*. It is called "The Vision From Which This Book Arose":

I had a dream: the wall of the centuries appeared
    to me.
It was of living flesh and unpolished granite,
An immobility made of uneasiness,
A building with the noise of crowds
5   Black holes starred with wild eyes,
Evolutions of monstrous groups,
Vast bas-reliefs, colossal frescoes;
Sometimes the wall opened, allowing rooms to be seen,
Caverns where the blessed were seated, and the
    powerful,
10   Conquerors besotted with crime, drunk on incense,
Interiors of gold, jasper, porphyry;
And this wall trembled like a tree in the west wind.
All the centuries, their brows bound with towers or
    ears of corn
Were there, sad sphinxes crouching on the enigma;
15   Each tier seemed vaguely alive;
It rose into the shadow, like an army
Petrified with its leader
At the moment it dared scale the night;

A block, it floated like a rolling cloud;
20   It was a great wall and it was a crowd;
Marble had scepter and blade in its fist,
The dust wept and the clay bled,
The stones that fell had a human form.
All humanity, with the unknown breath that leads it,
25   Undulating Eve, Adam floating, one and different,
Throbbed against this wall, and being, and the
            universe,
And destiny, the black thread that the tomb unwinds.
Sometimes lightning suddenly shone
Millions of faces on the livid wall.
30   I saw there this Nothing we call the All;
Kings, gods, glory and the law, the passing
Of generations downstream through the ages;
And before my gaze extended endless
Scourges, sufferings, ignorance, hunger,
35   Superstition, knowledge, history
Like a black façade disappearing from sight.

And this wall composed of all that crumbles
Rose up, steep-sloped, sad, formless. Where?
I do not know. In some place of shadows.

40   There are no mists, as there are no algebras,
That can resist, in depths of numbers or of heavens,
The calm, deep fixity of the eyes;
I observed this wall, at first confused and vague,
Whose form floated wave-like,
45   Where all seemed fog, vertigo, illusion;
And, beneath my thoughtful eye, the strange vision
Became less foggy and more clear in proportion
As my pupil grew less troubled and more sure.

Chaos of beings, rising from the chasm to the
            firmament,
50   All the monsters, each in his compartment,
The centuries — heartless, hideous, unclean.

Fog and reality! Cloud and map of the world!
This dream was history with open door. . . .

Presenting this poem in the Hachette edition, Ph. Van
Tieghen notes "the image of a building containing humanity's entire past is taken up again here." The poem unfolds
in imposing images that describe "the whole, black, vague,
limitless human wonder." "The Vision From Which This
Book Arose" is a great historical — "saturnine" let us say —
fresco. Beginning with creation, passing through Indian,
Persian, Hebrew, and Arabic civilizations, thence crossing
through Rome and the Middle Ages, it ends in the nineteenth century in order to cast light on the present.

Clarifying Hugo's experiences in the sphere of Saturn,
Steiner adds[63]:

It was like a fecundation of all this past, thanks to what
had been lived through in the Hibernian Mysteries, and
when this personality appeared anew on earth, it found
itself faced with the impulses which the evolution of its
soul would have to accomplish.

Let us note here the important indication that the poet's
soul found itself "faced" with impulses of the future. A detailed study of Hugo's biography would easily illustrate this
aspect of his destiny.

As the poem continues it confirms this inner struggle:

What titan painted this unheard-of thing?
120   On the bottomless wall of spreading shadow
Who sculpted the dream that was suffocating me?
What arm constructed with all the forfeits,
All the mourning, tears, and horrors,
This vast chain of living gloom?
125   This dream, I trembled from it, was a dark deed
Between creation and humanity;
Cries gushed forth from below the pillars;

Arms rising from the walls raised their fists to the stars;
The flesh was Gomorrah and the soul was Sion;
130   Vast thought! It was the confrontation
Of what we were with what we are.

It is astonishing in such a case how the text itself speaks!
Does not this poem convey an artistic experience by means
of which Hugo's experiences in the sphere of Saturn are
made transparent? Is it not the privilege of the artist, amongst
other things, to convey — by means of images, sounds, or
other materials — prenatal experiences? Think, for example,
of Plato's Dialogues.

In the poem we are quoting a true spiritual experience
obviously shows through. This can be seen in more than one
passage — for example in the following:

I contemplated the irons, the sensual delights, the evils,
115   The dead, the avatars, the metempsychoses,
And in the darkness hewn from beings and things,
I watched Satan prowl, this poacher in the forests
        of God,
Black, laughing, his eye on fire.

As a whole, the poem falls into two parts. The first, of
which we have already spoken, turns toward the past, in
conformity with Hugo's experiences in the sphere of Saturn.
The second opens powerfully toward the future, confirming
Steiner's words:

This soul [Hugo] had been turned toward the past in
the sphere of Saturn, and descended directly from there
onto the earth, and by virtue of the fact that the past
had been illuminated by initiation, this soul was a personality firmly established at the heart of earthly life,
but endowed with a vision of the future, a personality

in whom lived vast and potent ideas, impulses and great
feelings. . . .

That Victor Hugo was "a personality firmly established at
the heart of earthly life" is confirmed by the facts. Besides
his considerable work, which earned him a fortune, Hugo
was a member of the Acadèmie Française, a peer of France,
and a deputy in the National Assembly both after the revolu-
tion of 1848 and after the fall of the Second Empire. As
regards his fortune, Guillemin writes: "Eager and methodical,
[Hugo] made a fortune with his books and plays. . . . By
1885, his assets were worth about seven million francs." [64]

As for "vast and potent ideas, impulses and great feelings,"
they show through clearly in his poetry and prose. We need
only mention the poems "Open Sky (Plein Ciel)" and "Lux"
and of course *Les Miserables*. It is therefore not surprising to
find this in a critical review: "Under the simple aspect of the
palatine market-towns [Hugo] sought to uncover the secret
of the past and penetrate the enigma of the future." [65]

The second part of the poem corresponds to this metamorphosis of the past into the impulses of the future:

140   This wall, a block of funebrial darkness,
       Rose into the infinite one misty morning.
       Whitening by degrees on the distant horizon
       This somber vision, dark abridgement of the world,
       Would disappear in an immeasurable dawn,
145   And, begun at night, would finish in glimmering
             light.

We are coming to an astonishing passage of this muscular
poem, a passage that confirms Steiner's indications concerning Hugo's initiation. The first part of the poem has at-
tempted to paint in living colors, powerful words, and vary-
ing rhythms, humanity's past:

All peoples were there, having for platforms, all time;
55   All the temples, with dreams for steps;
Here the paladins, there the patriarchs;
Dodona whispering low to Membra;
And Thebes and Raphidim, and its sacred rock,
Where Aaron and Hur raised the two hands of Moses
60   On the Jews struggling for the promised land;
Amos' chariot of fire amid the hurricanes;
All these men, half princes, half brigands,
Transformed by fable with grace or anger,
Drowned in the shelves of popular tales,
65   Archangels, half-gods, hunters of men, heroes
Of the Eddas, the Vedas, the Romanceros;
Those whose sensuality stands up like a lance-head;
Those before whom the earth and the darkness are
          silent;
Saul, David; and Delphi, and the Cave of Endor
70   Whose flames are extinguished with scissors of
          gold;
Nimrod among the dead; Booz among the sheaves;
Divine Tiberiuses, great and proud, gathered together,
Displaying at Capri, in the forum, in camps,
Necklaces that Tacitus arranged in yokes;
75   The golden chain of the throne ending in prison.
This vast wall had slopes like a mountain.
O night! nothing was lacking this apparition.
All was there, matter, spirit, mud and light;
All the cities, Thebes, Athens, the stages of
80   Romes on the heaps of Tyres and Carthages;
All the rivers, the Scheldt, the Rhine, the Nile, the Aar,
The Rubicon, saying to someone who is Caesar,
"If you are still citizens, you are so
Only up to here." The hills rose up, black skeletons,
85   And on these hills horrible clouds wandered,
Phantoms dragging the moon amongst them.
The wall seemed to be shaken by the wind;
It was a crossing of flames and clouds,
Of mysterious games of clarity, of shadows

90   Sent back from century to century and from scepter
            to shield,
        Where India ends up being Germany,
        Where Solomon is reflected in Charlemagne;
        The whole human wonder, black, vague, unlimited;
        Freedom breaking immutability;
95   Horeb with the burnt hillsides, Pinda with the green
            slopes,
        Hicetas preceding Newton, discoveries
        Shaking their torch to the bottom of the sea,
        Jason on the dromon, Fulton on the steamer;
        The Marseillaise, Aeschylus, and the angel after the
            ghost;
100   Capaneus standing on the gate of Elektra;
        Bonaparte standing on the bridge of Lodi;
        Christ dying near where Nero is applauded. . . .

Now, after this tableau — this fresco — has been sketched
the poem seems like a giant sphere in which past and future
meet in a terrible collision. And we hear, echoing to infinity,
the groaning of the centuries.

        From the direction of dawn
        Passed the spirit of Orestes, with musky sound;
        And at the same time, from the direction of night,
        Frighted black genius fleeing in an eclipse,
160   Fearful came the immense Apocalypse;
        And their double thunder through the mist
        Approached on my right and on my left; and I was
            afraid
        As if taken between two chariots of shadow.

Orestes' spirit is the clarity of the Greek genius. The
Oresteia is the name of Aeschylus' trilogy which includes
Agamemnon, Elektra, and the Eumenides. From one direc-
tion then: the Oresteia, the past, Greek clarity, light, the

East, its decadence, dawn. From the other: the Apocalypse, struggles yet to come, prophecy, the coming of the Holy Spirit, the woman clad in the Sun. But where Hugo shows himself an initiate, a connoisseur of initiatory knowledge, is when he places the Oresteia at dawn, in the East, and the Apocalypse in the direction of night: this is a sign of authentic vision, for, intellectually, one's inclination would be to place the future in the dawn. However, the future builds itself in the darkness of night, in the living darkness of the will.[66]

> From the direction of dawn,
> *Passed* . . . the spirit of Orestes. . . .
> And at the same time, from the direction of night,
> Frighted black genius fleeing in an eclipse
> Fearful *came* the immense Apocalypse. . . .

How to understand this fundamental inversion? What are the true qualities of Light and Darkness? Steiner writes:

> What is above all important today is the fact that the universe, including humanity, is a complex structure of thought-light, of light-thought, of will-matter, and of matter-will, and that what presents itself to us in a concrete way has been built up and formed in accordance with infinitely varied combinations of light-thought, thought-light, matter-will, and will-matter. Therefore, if we want to understand it, we must observe the cosmos from a qualitative point of view and not just a quantitative one. Then we see that it includes an element of continual death: a dying away of the past in light and a birth of the future in darkness.[67]

To all these ideas whose resonance reaches us through the density of the verse another feature is added, a dark flash, illuminating a sign in this vision, sealing its authenticity. Faced with this vision of the past which melts in the light, this vision of the future rising from the darkness, this contact with these two currents of humanity, what does the poet feel?

> . . . and I was afraid. . . .

Here we recognize the seal of a true experience of Apocalypse, of the future, of devouring Time. Facing the past there is no fear, because the past is congealed in the light, is dead, having become an object of contemplation:

> And beneath my thoughtful eye the strange vision
> Became less foggy. . . .

In the face of a vision of the future, however, fear lies in wait. The seal of what is true, authentic in an experience of darkness is fear. In a lecture called *Thought and Will as Darkness and Light*, Steiner characterizes the past and the future, completing their forms as light-past and darkness-future, in the following way: "When they felt the past decaying in light, the ancient Persians, with their instinctive clairvoyance, called it Ahura Mazda, and when they felt the future forming in the darkness they called it Ahriman." [68]

Did Hugo have a presentiment of this? Or did he perhaps even have knowledge of the spiritual, existential situation of human beings who are placed in the center of this conflict? The following poem answers this question:

> Don't think, darkness, that I tremble
> Because you come at evening to wall the skies;
> I hear voices speaking quietly in the shadows
> And I feel gazes upon me but see no eyes;
>
> Yet I have faith! Ahriman fears Zarathustra;
> The more darkness comes, the more the wise man
>   loves and believes,

And before the luminous greatness the star gives
To the good prophet, the evil god grows less.

Despite yourself, you are crossed with rays;
Hope is mixed with your livid terrors;
Beneath your outstretched wings you do not disturb us
Any more than the crows shake the belfry.

O darkness, the sky is a gloomy precinct
Whose door you close, and whose key the soul owns;
And night divides itself in half, being diabolical and
        holy,
Between Iblis, the black angel, and Christ, the starry
Human Being.[69]

Ahriman, spirit linked to matter, characterizes himself as the Father of Fear. This follows clearly from a passage, from one of Steiner's Mystery Dramas, which we shall now quote. Before we do so, however, some explanation is perhaps in order. Transposing anthroposophy into the artistic domain, between 1910 and 1913 Steiner wrote four Mystery Dramas, which were performed annually at the Anthroposophic Congress then held in Munich. The order of these dramas was as follows:

The Portal of Initiation   1910

The Soul's Probation   1911

The Guardian of the Threshold   1912

The Soul's Awakening   1913

The course of these four dramas depicts the evolution of the characters toward an ever-deepening knowledge of life, a knowledge that leads them to perceive, as they penetrate the facts of daily life, inspiring spiritual impulses. In this way, for example, the various trials and crises that are passed through tear away the veil of maya or illusion in them, with the result that gradually they become conscious of the reality of reincarnation — for the trials and crises are linked to acts committed in a previous life. Hence a person's biography is not the product of chance, but is woven from subtle threads of silver and gold — silver for the determination of effect by cause, gold for the space of freedom that is reserved for every human being. At the same time a more exact, living knowledge of the adversary forces, of evil, deepens in them. There is not only simply evil, but two aspects of evil, two real Beings who oppose human beings in their struggle to realize the Good. These two Spirits bear the names of Lucifer, the Light Bearer, and Ahriman, the Spirit of Darkness.

In relation to the problem of fear which occupies us now, here is what Ahriman himself says in one of Steiner's dramas:

> In rank I was once equal to the gods.
> But they curtailed perforce my ancient rights.
> I wish to mold the human beings so
> for Brother Lucifer and his realm
> that each could only show himself
> in spirit realms as equal among equals,
> a model only, never
> a ruler over beings.
> I wanted therefore to give strength to man
> to prove himself to Lucifer as equal.
> And had I stayed within the realm of gods
> this would have happened in primeval times.
> The gods, however, willed to be the rulers upon earth;
> they had to ban my power
> out of their realm into the deep abyss
> that I should not empower men too strongly.
> Now only from this region am I able
> to send my mighty power toward the earth.
> It turns, however, on the way to . . . fear.[70]

John, in his Apocalypse, also communicates this experience of the fear he endures — this fear or anguish before the future which is about to be unveiled to him in the great images that we know so well: "And he had in his right hand seven stars; and out of his mouth went a sharp two-edged sword: and his countenance was as the sun shineth in his strength. And when I saw him, I fell at his feet as dead. And he laid his right hand on me, saying unto me, Fear not." [71]

Let us recall that the Mysteries of Saturn inspire dread, a strong feeling of tragedy, a dramatic emotion. Steiner writes: "Whoever gradually learns through initiation-knowledge to perceive the Saturn-mysteries . . . undergoes experiences of dramatic intensity, shattering experiences, that are harder and harder to bear because these experiences strike at the very roots of life." [72]

When we remember that history is woven of the struggle of two currents, one coming from the past, the other from the future — the second continually destroying the first — the poet's vision acquires a still greater exactitude, a more startling prominence, a more direct truthfulness. The current of the past, the light, the current of what has become — what has been stopped, formed — must sooner or later undergo the destructive effect of the other current, that of the future. It is the eternal "Battle of the Ancients against the Moderns." The will-force of Ahriman attacks and constantly destroys the human accomplishments that Lucifer would conserve and install in eternity.

"This is the struggle of day against night," murmured Hugo in his agony.

At bottom, the fact of finding oneself placed in the current of Time, of feeling it profoundly within oneself, of living the metamorphosis of the past into the future, of being at the junction where the future pulverizes the past to emerge in new forms, is always a terrifying experience. Let us read carefully the passage in the poem where Hugo witnesses the Oresteia and the Apocalypse:

     They passed. There was a dark agitation.
165   The first spirit cried: Fate!
     The second cried: God! And dark eternity
     Repeated these cries in funereal echo.

This terrifying passage shook the shadows;
Everything tottered at the noise they made; the wall,
170   Full of shadows, shuddered; everything took part;
        the king
Put his hand on his helmet, the idol on his miter;
The whole vision trembled like a pane of glass,
And broke, falling into the night in pieces;
And when the two spirits, like two great birds,
175   Were fled, in the strange fog of the idea,
The pale vision reappeared full of cracks,
Like a ruined temple with gigantic shafts,
That let one see the abyss between its crazy quilt
        of walls.

Here we have creative imagination, precision and truth of poetic vision. After the passage of the *two* Spirits, the devastation to thinking is great and deep. The next line puts it admirably:

Instead of a universe, there was a cemetery.

Saturn, the spirit of death — Chronos, Time devouring its children — such are the thoughts that visit us as we read this part of the poem.

This experience of Time the Devourer that Hugo gives us recalls another great image, also described in pictures rich in artistic value and philosophy. It is the experience Arjuna has in the Bhagavad Gita when in a moment of trial he asks his Master to manifest himself to him, saying, "I would see your divine form and body. Show me your imperishable being, O master of Yoga, if you think I can see it."

Then Krishna agrees to show himself in his reality and says: "What you must see, your human eye can never see; but there is a divine eye, and this eye, here, I give it to you. Contemplate me and my divine Yoga."

Krishna gives to his beloved disciple the possibility of seeing him. He gives Arjuna the spiritual eye — spiritual sight — that will allow him to see Krishna in his essence, in his majesty. What does Arjuna see?

"I see you — touching the heavens, dazzling, of many colors. Your open mouths and your enormous flaming eyes. Troubled and in pain is the soul within me, and I can find neither peace nor joy."

Once again we discover here the intense emotions which seize the soul when it confronts these spheres. For what in fact does Arjuna see? How does he himself characterize the powerful being before whom he finds himself and whose real Being he is contemplating?

"As I behold your terrible mouths, with their many destructive defenses, your countenances which are as the fires of *death* and *time*, I lose my sense of direction and cannot find peace. Bend your heart to me with mercy, O God of gods, refuge of all worlds."

Troubled by this terrible vision, Arjuna asks in anguish: "Tell me who you are, you who are clothed in this terrible form? I salute you, great Divinity. I would know who you are, you who have been from the beginning, for I do not know the shape of your works."

This burning question is answered by a roar of thunder.

"I am the Spirit of Time which destroys all things, and I have come here raised up in my vast form to destroy these peoples. Even without you, all the warriors facing you must die." [73]

In this beautiful passage, one phrase above all, perhaps, strikes us: "I am the spirit of time . . . raised up . . . to destroy these peoples." Reading it, how can we not think of Hugo's poem?

The Legend of the Centuries — note the title — is the book which emerged from this vision. It is the product of the poet's genial intuition which, in a single glance, takes in the whole of history, above all its past, but also its movement, its metamorphoses:

Out of the deep, heavy impression left
By this chaos of life on my gloomy thought,
Out of this vision of the movement of humanity
210   This book, where beside yesterday we glimpse
tomorrow,
Has arisen, reflecting from poem to poem
All this ghastly, dizzy clarity.

The past holds the major place, but the future too is sketched out: "beside yesterday we glimpse tomorrow." For example, the poem "Open Sky":

The pure Spirits of the August Empyrean,
Before this dark globe growing light,
No longer feel the bleeding of the love they have in
them.
A clarity appears in their beautiful dark look,
And the Archangel begins to smile in the shadow.[74]

Thanks to the indications given by spiritual science — anthroposophy — the life of a person of genius, which is often complex, and always enigmatic, becomes clearer. The fresco we have examined, these sometimes obscure images, which have made the poet misunderstood and frequently treated, sometimes with intelligent irony, sometimes maliciously, as a visionary, a "magus" — this fresco was drawn by him from the depths of his Hibernian initiate's soul or else, as here, from the engraved memory of his sojourn in the sphere of Saturn. He felt in himself more than he could consciously grasp:

I do not know myself. I am veiled from myself.
God alone knows who I am and what I am called.[75]

Or, again, this cry:

Of the sun, my former country.[76]

Did his contemporaries understand him? Whilst the anony-
mous crowd of readers felt his greatness and all his books
were bestsellers, many of those whom we now call intellectu-
als were his bitter opponents. Here, as an example, is an
extract from an article that appeared while he was alive and
that attacks him in high style: "These are vague impressions
which cannot be analyzed, that we cannot touch with our
senses; these are experiences with this language that never
revolts against him and which he can shape to all his fanta-
sies; images which clash against each other and produce
other images . . . finally something that cannot be defined
and which has no reality — a capital defect in a work of
art." [77] Let us note the reproach: "which cannot be analyzed,
which we cannot touch with our senses."

Another critic (Rivet) treats Hugo as "naive," while Zola,
after reading "The Ass," explodes, "A wager made against
French genius!" — declaring to the *Figaro* that Hugo is
nothing but a "senile old man." [78] A. de Pontmartin speaks
of "mental alienation." And *La Croix*, the well-known catholic
journal, can close this list by adding: "He [Hugo] was mad
for thirty years." [79] But Hugo himself had already written:
"A man is dead, but insult does not cease for so little. Hate
eats his corpse."

Others, however, including his great contemporaries, and
above all Baudelaire, admired him: "According to what com-
bination of historical circumstances, philosophical destinies
and sidereal conjunctions this man was born among us, I
don't know." [80] This connects directly to Steiner's statement:
"We really only understand another human being when we
consider him or her in relation to the evolution that has been
undergone between death and a new birth." Is not this
constant reproach of "lack of intelligence" or analytic spirit

simply a lack of intuition on the part of these critics? Don't we know that the Hibernian Mysteries were "especially profound, not in an intellectual but in an intensely human sense?"

Let us conclude this brief study of the poem "Vision From Which This Book Arose" with a passage that resonates particularly fully with the experiences undergone by Victor Hugo:

> This book is the terrifying remnant of the Tower of
>   Babel,
> The mournful tower of things, the building
> Of good and evil, of tears, of mourning, of sacrifice,
> Once proud, dominating distant horizons,
> Today possessing only hideous stumps,
> Scattered, fallen, lost in the dark valley;
> It is the bitter, immense, broken-down epic of
>   humanity — crumbled away.

Appendix to Chapter II

Vision From Which This Book Arose
(Complete)

I had a dream: the wall of the centuries appeared to
me.

It was of living flesh and unpolished granite,
An immobility made of uneasiness,
A building with the noise of crowds,
5 Black holes starred with wild eyes,
Evolutions of monstrous groups,
Vast bas-reliefs, colossal frescoes;
Sometimes the wall opened, allowing rooms to be seen,
Caverns where the blessed were seated, and the
            powerful,
10 Conquerors besotted with crime, drunk on incense,
Interiors of gold, jasper, porphyry;
And this wall trembled like a tree in the west wind.
All the centuries, their brows bound with towers or
            ears of grain,
Were there, sad sphinxes crouching on the enigma;
15 Each tier seemed vaguely alive;
It rose into the shadow, like an army
Petrified with its leader
At the moment it dared scale the Night;
A block, it floated like a rolling cloud;
20 It was a great wall and it was a crowd;
Marble had the scepter and blade in its fist,
The dust wept and the clay bled,
The stones that fell had a human form.
All humanity, with the unknown breath that leads it,

25   Undulating Eve, Adam floating, one and different,
        Throbbed against this wall, and being, and the
              universe,
        And destiny, the black thread that the tomb unwinds.
        Sometimes lightning suddenly shone
        Millions of faces on the livid wall.
30   I saw there this Nothing we call the All;
        Kings, gods, glory and the law, the passing
        Of generations downstream through the ages;
        And before my gaze extended endless
        Scourges, sufferings, ignorance, hunger,
35   Superstition, knowledge, history
        Like a black façade disappearing from sight.

        And this wall composed of all that crumbles
        Rose up, steep-sloped, sad, formless. Where?
        I do not know. In some place of shadows.

40   There are no mists, as there are no algebras,
        That can resist, in depths of numbers or of heavens,
        The calm, deep fixity of the eyes;
        I observed this wall, at first confused and vague,
        Whose form floated wave-like,
45   Where all seemed fog, vertigo, illusion;
        And, beneath my thoughtful eye, the strange vision
        Became less foggy and more clear in proportion
        As my pupil grew less troubled and more sure.

        Chaos of beings, rising from the chasm to the
              firmament,
50   All the monsters, each in his compartment,
        The centuries — heartless, hideous, unclean.
        Fog and reality! Cloud and map of the world!
        This dream was history with open doors.
        All peoples were there, having for platforms, all time;
55   All the temples, with dreams for steps;
        Here the paladins, there the patriarchs;
        Dodona whispering low to Membra;
        And Thebes and Raphidim, and its sacred rock,

Where Aaron and Hur raised the two hands of Moses
60   On the Jews struggling for the promised land;
Amos' chariot of fire amid the hurricanes;
All these men, half princes, half brigands,
Transformed by fable with grace or anger,
Drowned in the shelves of popular tales,
65   Archangels, half-gods, hunters of men, heroes
Of the Eddas, the Vedas, the Romanceros;
Those whose sensuality stands up like a lance-head;
Those before whom the earth and the darkness are
        silent;
Saul, David; and Delphi, and the Cave of Endor
70   Whose flames are extinguished with scissors of
        gold;
Nimrod among the dead; Booz among the sheaves;
Divine Tiberiuses, great and proud, gathered together,
Displaying at Capri, in the forum, in camps,
Necklaces that Tacitus arranged in yokes;
75   The golden chain of the throne ending in prison.
This vast wall had slopes like a mountain.
O night! nothing was lacking this apparition.
All was there, matter, spirit, mud and light;
All the cities, Thebes, Athens, the stages of
80   Romes on the heaps of Tyres and Carthages;
All the rivers, the Scheldt, the Rhine, the Nile, the Aar,
The Rubicon, saying to someone who is Caesar,
"If you are still citizens, you are so
Only up to here." The hills rose up, black skeletons,
85   And on these hills horrible clouds wandered,
Phantoms dragging the moon amongst them.
The wall seemed to be shaken by the wind;
It was a crossing of flames and clouds,
Of mysterious games of clarity, of shadows
90   Sent back from century to century and from scepter
        to shield,
Where India ends up being Germany,
Where Solomon is reflected in Charlemagne;
The whole human wonder, black, vague, unlimited;
Freedom breaking immutability;

95   Horeb with the burnt hillsides, Pinda with the green
           slopes
      Hicetas preceding Newton, discoveries
      Shaking their torch to the bottom of the sea,
      Jason on the dromon, Fulton on the steamer;
      The Marseillaise, Aeschylus, and the angel after the
           ghost;
100   Capaneus standing on the gate of Elektra;
      Bonaparte standing on the bridge of Lodi;
      Christ dying near where Nero is applauded.
      Here is the fearful way of the throne, this paving
      Of murder, fury, war, slavery;
105   Herd-humanity! howling
      Committing crimes on a dreary and gloomy peak,
      Striking, blaspheming, suffering,
      Alas! I hear, beneath my feet, in the abyss,
      Misery sobbing with dull groans,
110   Of dark incurable mouth, ever complaining.
      And on the mournful vision, and on myself,
      Whom I saw as at the bottom of a tarnished mirror,
      Immense life opened its misshapen branches;
      I contemplated the irons, the sensual delights, the evils,
115   The dead, the avatars, the metempsychoses,
      And in the darkness hewn from beings and things,
      I watched Satan prowl, this poacher in the forests
           of God,
      Black, laughing, his eye on fire.

      What titan painted this unheard-of thing?
120   On the bottomless wall of spreading shadow
      Who sculpted the dream that was suffocating me?
      What arm constructed with all the forfeits,
      All the mourning, tears, and horrors,
      This vast chain of living gloom?
125   This dream, I trembled from it, was a dark deed
      Between creation and humanity;
      Cries gushed forth from below the pillars;
      Arms rising from the walls raised their fists to the stars;
      The flesh was Gomorrah and the soul was Sion;

130   Vast thought! It was the confrontation
        Of what we were with what we are;
        Beasts, by divine right, mingled with humans,
        As in a hell, or in a paradise;
        Crimes raged there, enlarged by their shadows;
135   And even the ugliness was not unbecoming
        To the tragic horror of these giant frescoes.
        And I saw there the ancient forgotten time.
        I plumbed it. Good was connected with evil
        As vertebra is joined to vertebra.

140   This wall, a block of funebrial darkness,
        Rose into the infinite one misty morning.
        Whitening by degrees on the distant horizon,
        This somber vision, dark abridgement of the world,
        Would disappear in an immeasurable dawn,
145   And, begun at night, would finish in glimmering
           light.

        Sad day seemed there like pale sweat;
        And this shapeless silhouette was veiled
        With a misty spiral of starred smoke.

        While I dreamed, my eye fixed on this wall
150   Sown with souls, covered with a darkened movement
        And the wild gestures of a ghostly people,
        A rumor passed beneath the murky domes,
        I heard two deep noises, coming from the sky
        In the opposite direction to the depth of eternal
           silence;
155   The firmament that none can open or close
        Seemed about to part.

        From the direction of dawn
        Passed the spirit of Orestes, with musky sound;
        And at the same time, from the direction of night,
        Frighted black genius fleeing in an eclipse,
160   Fearful came the immense Apocalypse;
        And their double thunder through the mist

Approached on my right and on my left; and I was
    afraid
As if taken between two chariots of shadow.
They passed. There was a dark agitation.
165 The first spirit cried: Fate!
The second cried: God! And dark eternity
Repeated these cries in funereal echo.
This terrifying passage shook the shadows;
Everything tottered at the noise they made; the wall,
170 Full of shadows, shuddered; everything took part;
    the king
Put his hand on his helmet, the idol his on his miter;
The whole vision trembled like a pane of glass,
And broke, falling into the night in pieces;
And when the two spirits, like two great birds,
175 Were fled, in the strange fog of the idea,
The pale vision reappeared full of cracks,
Like a ruined temple with gigantic shafts,
That let one see the abyss between its crazy quilt
    of walls.

When I saw it again, after the two angels
180 Had broken it by the shock of their strange wings,
There was no longer this prodigious wall, entire,
Where fate coupled with infinity,
Where all times gathered together joined with ours,
Where the centuries could question one another,
185 Without one making a mistake and failing in the
    summons;
Instead of a continent, there was an archipelago;
Instead of a universe, there was a cemetery;
Here and there a dismal stone rose up,
Some standing pillar, no longer bearing anything;
190 All the mutilated centuries were stranded; without
    a link;
Each epoch hung demolished; none
Was without a rip, without a hole,
And everywhere stagnant shadows and pools of night
Rotted on the wreckage of the past.

195 Amid the mists where my eye fell was only
     The deformed, tottering debris of a dream,
     Having the vague appearance of an intermittent bridge
     Falling arch by arch into the waiting abyss,
     Like a fleet in distress that's foundering;
200 Resembling a dark and interrupted phrase
     The hurricane, this stutterer wandering on the
          summits,
     Always begins without ever finishing.

     Only the future continued to open
     On these black vestiges gilded by a pale orient
205 To rise like a star, amidst a cloud
     Where, without seeing thunder, one felt the presence
          of God.

     Out of the deep, heavy impression left
     By this chaos of life on my gloomy thought,
     Out of this vision of the movement of humanity
210 This book, where beside yesterday we glimpse
          tomorrow,
     Has arisen, reflecting from poem to poem
     All this ghastly, dizzy clarity.

     This book is the terrifying remnant of the Tower of
          Babel,
235 The mournful tower of things, the building
     Of good and evil, of tears, of mourning, of sacrifice,
     Once proud, dominating distant horizons,
     Today possessing only hideous stumps,
     Scattered, fallen, lost in the dark valley;
240 This is the bitter, immense, broken-down epic of
          humanity — crumbled away.

                              (Guernsey, April 26, 1857)

III

Hugo,
Initiate of the Hibernian Mysteries

Initiated in a past life, Hugo could not speak, in the full light of consciousness, of the truths he had lived formerly in the sanctuaries of initiation. The impulses that moved his soul and are translated into the magic of his words, the incantatory power of his images, remained hidden to him. Did he have any idea of them? Did he not feel bubbling up in his soul the powerful experiences that he had lived during his initiation?

At the end of his life, he confided to A. Houssaye who was dining with him one January evening in 1874: "For half a century I have been writing my thoughts in prose and in verse but I know that I have written but a thousandth part of what is within me." [81] How then does it happen that it is so difficult today for an initiate to recover consciously his memories of initiation? What veils from him his past experiences which we know were so powerful, "magnificent," and "sublime"?

The hardness of our present bodies, as well as our materialist education, constitute the obstacles posed by the present historical moment of evolution. Only energetic discipline, conscious spiritual development, can break the narrow circle in which, from childhood on, human beings today find themselves imprisoned. Therefore the greatness of our poet in this life, in the nineteenth century, was to be a writer of genius, an artist of the first order, whose voice resounded intensely throughout the century. Nevertheless we may suspect that, though veiled, the experiences he lived through in Ireland penetrated his work. Therefore we may try to read in it the history of this great soul and its trials.

Let us once again try to apply the method chosen in the first half of this work — without, to begin with, judging the validity of the claims of Spiritual Science. Let us seek out patiently in the work of the poet revealing traces of the initiation that Spiritual Science tells us took place in Ireland. Let us place side by side the description of the trials undergone by a disciple aspiring to initiation in former times and certain parts of Hugo's work. Perhaps, if we do so, light will burst forth and we will be convinced. We shall then truly encounter the poet through his work — his eternal individuality as it expresses itself through different incarnations. As we start, let us allow to live once more before our souls one essential feature of this Hibernian Initiation: namely, the fact that "the knowledge possessed by these Irish Mysteries was especially profound, not in an intellectual but in an intensely human sense."

We begin with the oft-quoted lines with which Hugo defines himself:

The century was two years old! Rome replaced Sparta,
Napoleon was already breaking through beneath
            Bonaparte,
Already here and there the Emperor's brow
Shattered the first Consul's narrow mask.
Then was born, in Besancon, an old Spanish town,
Tossed like a seed at the whim of the soaring air,
Of blood mixed of both Brittainy and Lorraine,
A colorless child, lackluster, voiceless;
Weak he was, like a dream,
Abandoned by all except his mother,
And his neck, bent like a weak reed,
Served at once as his coffin and his cradle.
This child, whom life wiped from its book,
Who had not even a tomorrow to live,
Was I — . . . .

If sometimes my thoughts fly from my breast,
My songs scattered in shreds by the world;

If it pleases me to hide love and pain
In a corner of some ironic, mocking novel;
If I shake the stage with my imagination,
If I shock in the eyes of a crowd chosen
Of like minds, all living simultaneously
On my breath and speaking to the people with my
          voice;
If my head, a furnace where my spirit burns,
Tosses steely verses that boil and smoke
In a deep rhythm, a mysterious mold,
From which stanzas soar with open wings
          into the skies —
It is because love, the grave, glory, life,
Wave succeeding wave, wave by wave incessantly
          pursued,
Every breath, every ray, propitious or fatal,
Polishes and vibrates my crystal soul,
The myriad-voiced soul that the God I adore
Placed in the center of all like a deep-toned echo![82]

How does the poet feel, how does he define himself? Like an immense remembrance rising from the depths of memory, he sees himself a "crystal" sphere, the reflection of all possible experiences, "the center of all, a deep-toned echo."

In relation to this, let us consider the quality and intensity of the Irish initiatory experiences as conveyed by Rudolf Steiner in his lecture, "The Hibernian Mysteries."[83] Steiner tells us that one of the cultic experiences available to the candidate for initiation was the following. After having been long and patiently taught to experience every doubt and to recognize the deceptive nature of earthly truths, the disciple was given an experience of something that could only be fully experienced in images: he was led before two gigantic statues; one of these seemed to be made of some elastic substance, but inside it was hollow; majestic in size, it produced in one who saw it a profound impression.

The pupil of the Mysteries then had to meditate before this statue. It represented the solar, masculine principle. The pupil had to give himself intensely to the awe-inspiring gamut of emotions that he felt. A kind of rigid numbness of the soul then overtook him — "a numbness of the soul which felt like a bodily numbness as well." This new bodily and psychic state caused a change of consciousness. Steiner says: "The pupil felt that in this state his consciousness was entirely filled with the sensation of numbness. Then he felt that what was numb and frozen — namely, he himself — was being taken up into the Cosmic All. He felt as if he were being transported into the wide spaces of the Cosmos. And he could say to himself: The Cosmos is taking me into itself!"

And then came a remarkable experience [Steiner continues] — his consciousness was not extinguished but transformed. When this experience of frozen numbness and of being taken up into the Cosmic All had lasted a sufficient length of time — and this was ensured by the Initiators — the pupil could say to himself something to this effect: The rays of the Sun and the Stars are drawing me out into the Cosmic All, but nevertheless I remain here, within my own being. . . . When this experience had lasted for the necessary length of time, a remarkable vista came before the pupil. Now for the first time he realized the purpose of this state of consciousness which had set in during the numbness. For now, through his various experiences and their echoes, manifold impressions of winter landscapes came before him. . . . And during this experience he felt as though he were not actually in his body, but certainly in his sense organs; he felt that he was living with the whole of his being in his eyes, in his ears, also on the surface of his skin. And then, when his whole sense of feeling and touch seemed to be spread over his skin, he also felt: I have become like the elastic but hollow statue. He felt an intimate union between his eyes, for instance, and these landscapes. He felt as though in each eye the whole landscape at which he gazed was working, as though his eyes were an inner mirror reflecting everything outside him.

Is it a coincidence that this description of the feelings experienced by the pupil in the Hibernian Mysteries finds a parallel in Hugo's lines?

> Every breath, every ray, propitious or fatal,
> Polishes and vibrates my crystal soul.

Did not Steiner say that the winter landscapes that the pupil contemplated appeared to work in each eye as if the eye were an interior mirror reflecting everything outside of him . . . that he had become like the elastic, but hollow, statue?

Recall Hugo's lines:

> The myriad-voiced soul that the God I adore
> Placed in the center of all like a deep-toned echo!

After the experience of the elastic, but hollow statue the candidate for initiation, by means of an intimate but solely mental experience, becomes the hollow statue itself. He feels reflected in his soul, as though in a mirror, all that happens outside. Is not the crystal soul, of which Hugo speaks, porous and transparent to all that comes to it through the senses from without? Every breath, every ray polishes and vibrates his soul. The poet's experience becomes even more precise when it becomes identified with a "deep-toned echo," thereby irresistibly suggesting an openness to inspiration, to hearing the Harmony of the Spheres.

The reflection of the universe, of sounds and resonant waves, both by image and by the Harmony of the Spheres — thus Hugo feels himself to be, thus he defines himself:

> The myriad-voiced soul that the God I adore
> Placed at the center of all like a deep-toned echo!

"The Cosmos is taking me into itself" is Steiner's characterization of the Hibernian disciple's experience. Coincidence or reminiscence? Chance or the intuition of a past life?

Baudelaire, who was the most suited of Hugo's contemporaries to sense the profound impulses that welled up in the poet's soul, wrote: "The music of Hugo's lines fits with the deep harmonies of nature. A sculptor, he carved in his verses the unforgettable form of things; a painter, he illumined them with their own colors. . . . " [84] But Baudelaire goes further in his insight when he writes: "No artist is more universal than he, more fitted to come into contact with the forces of universal life, more disposed to bathe unendingly in nature."

The Hibernian initiate felt: "the rays of the Sun and the Stars are drawing me out into the Cosmic All . . ."

Baudelaire's genius sensed a cosmic element in Hugo. He goes on to describe how Hugo had "a uniquely broad ability to be absorbed in outer life." Better: "His subtle senses revealed to him abysses. He saw mysteries everywhere."

And what is to be said of the remark of a critic who wrote that Hugo was quite simply a man — "porous to the universe" and endowed with the ability "to make us really and vitally present both to ourselves and to the cosmos" — by whom creation "was reintegrated into the cosmos."

In this way an encounter with the poet's profound Being, his eternal individuality, slowly takes shape. We can go further still by considering, in the light of spiritual science, other aspects, other experiences of the initiatory schools of the Hibernian Mysteries. Again, Steiner:

It will be clear to you from the description of Initiation in the Hibernian Mysteries that the goal was to achieve insight into the secrets of cosmic and human existence, for the experiences of which I told you were of very far reaching importance for man's life of soul. Everything that is to lead him into the spiritual world depends upon conquests achieved as the result of crucial inner experiences and upon such a radical strengthening of his powers that in one way or another he succeeds in penetrating into that world.[85]

Let us now find another poem that reflects such formerly cultivated feelings, feelings born of this "insight into the secrets of cosmic and human existence." The poet's rich and prolific *oeuvre* gives us an abundant harvest from which to choose. Our attention, however, will be particularly drawn by a poem that precisely works this double mystery of outer nature or cosmos and inner human nature.

Have you ever, calm and quiet,
Climbed a mountain in the presence of the skies?
. . . .
Calm and quiet, have you listened?
. . . .
Gradually I distinguished, confused and veiled,
Two voices in this voice, mixed one with the other,
Voices of the earth and the seas overflowing to the sky,
Who sang together a universal song;
I distinguished them in the deep murmur
As one sees two currents cross beneath a wave.

One came from the seas: Hymn of glory! Happy hymn!
This was the voice of the billows speaking with each
          other;
The other, which rose from the earth where we are,
Was sad; it was the murmur of humanity;
And in this great concert, which sang night and day,
Each wave had its voice, every human being his sound.
. . . .
Brothers! Of these two strange, unbelievable voices,
Ceaselessly rising, endlessly disappearing,
That the Eternal listens to during eternity,
One said: NATURE! And the other said:
          HUMANITY!

Then I meditated; my faithful spirit

> Never, alas! had spread greater wings;
> Never in my shade had more day shone;
> I dreamed long, contemplating turn and turn about, ·
> After the dark abyss that the billows hid from me,
> The other, bottomless abyss that opened
>   in my soul. . . .[86]

Two poles are clearly indicated: Nature and Humanity. The poet feels himself before two abysses, exactly like the disciple of the Hibernian Mysteries. In Steiner's words, candidates for initiation "were thus led on the one hand to the edge of an abyss, and on the other to the edge of another abyss." [87] The abyss of self-knowledge and the abyss of the knowledge of nature.

> After the dark abyss that the billows hid from me,
> The other, bottomless abyss that opened in my soul.

Two mysteries, two sufferings, two existential struggles. The trials of the candidate for initiation are great and victories are acquired at great suffering. Carried away on "The Slope of Reverie," Hugo lets us into his confidence:

> Friends, don't dig into your reveries;
> Don't search the soil of your flowery plains;
> And when a sleeping ocean is offered to your gaze,
> Swim on the surface or play on the shore.
> For thought is dark! An invisible slope
> Runs from the real world to the invisible sphere;
> The spiral is deep, and when one descends there
> It endlessly extends itself, growing ever larger,
> And for having touched some fatal enigma,
> You often return from this gloomy journey pale
>   and wan.

The poem ends with these breathless words:

> My spirit then dove beneath this unknown wave,
> To the depth of the abyss it swam naked and alone,
> Moving endlessly from the ineffable to the invisible. . . .
> Suddenly, with a terrible cry, it returned
> Startled, breathless, stupid, terrified,
> For at the bottom it had found eternity.

Steiner says more calmly: "Only one who has truly practiced the struggle for knowledge knows what must be undergone and what was thus proposed to the pupils of the Hibernian Mysteries."

Let us go further into Hugo's soul and contemplate, with all the respect and admiration such an act requires, the trials, expressed in living images, he went through after his initiation. Can a poet unveil his soul with the utmost transparency, can he with the utmost frankness and openness express the hidden riches that live in him? Certainly he can when he speaks with true art, when he sings his poetry — his poetic experience — when he sings the joy of creativity, of impregnating his word with the substance of his soul.

> If they tell you that art and poetry
> Are an eternal stream of banal ambrosia,
> That they are noise, the crowd, attached to your feet,
> Or the idle fantasy of a gilded salon,
> Or rime in flight by rime apprehended,
> O don't believe it!
>
> O sacred poets, wild, sublime,
> Go, spread your souls upon the peaks
> On snowy summits exposed to icy blasts
> In holy deserts where your spirit recollects itself
> In woods that autumn carries off leaf by leaf,
> On sleeping lakes in the shadow of glens![88]

This poem, "Pan," was written on November 8, 1831, when the poet was twenty-nine. It is a profession of poetic faith. In it, Hugo confides his deepest thought. Here is how one critic characterizes this poem: "Poetry, for the romantic poet, is not a game but the exercise of a vital function which consists in a broad and enthusiastic communion with all the forms of the universe. He effectuates in himself a permanent exchange between the interior and exterior worlds. This faculty of communing with the cosmos, with a universe in which each thing is a reflection of divinity, makes a sacred being of the poet." These phrases perfectly characterize the content of the poem, "Pan." How alive Hugo's images are!

> O sacred poets, wild, sublime,
> Go, spread your souls upon the peaks.

Such lines, however, could remain simply poetic images, beautiful, harmonious rhythms but finally without the additional weight, the spiritual dimension of which our souls today have an inkling, a need. It is at this point that spiritual science can enter in, casting a bright light on the poet's feelings, showing these to be a living memory of an initiatory path. With this, we are placed in quite another perspective. It is no longer necessary to torture the lines of the poem. Quite by themselves they resonate with past experiences. What were these experiences?

Let us remember this: after having had the experiences with the male statue, which was elastic but hollow, the student of the Hibernian Mysteries was led before a second, female statue: "This statue was composed of a different material; it was plastic, not elastic, and extremely soft." (In fact, the student was led before both statues simultaneously but the different feelings and experiences in relation to these statues may be separated.) The first statue represented the Sun and Science, the second revealed the Mysteries of the Moon and Art. As we have seen, the first statue led to a numbing of consciousness, followed by an experience of the annihilation of the student's being, which was accompanied by dreams of winter. The second statue made the student feel the power of artistic creation — but stripped of truth, subject to illusion, error, chance, in brief, to personal subjectivity. This experience was accompanied by dreams of summer. The second statue seemed to say to the pupil: I am (fantasy), but what I am (my being) has no truth.

"Thus two statues stood before the student, one of whom represented ideas without being, the other images of fantasy without truth. . . ."

What the statues said:

First statue.
I am the image of the World,
Behold, how I lack being.
I live in thy Knowledge,
I now become in thee Avowal.

Second statue.
I am the image of the World
Behold, how I lack truth.
If thou wilt dare to live with me,
I will be thy comfort.[89]

Before the second statue the pupil is posed a fundamental question that we may briefly characterize as follows: how can one overcome the lack of truth in artistic images, in fantasy images that have no truth? Before the first statue, being is lacking, the substance is not in the form; but before the second statue, the content is not shaped by clear outlines, by what is true. The answer to this problem, this riddle arising on the pupil's inner path, will illuminate the depths of the poem "Pan." What is the answer?

"The pupil had come to know that the tendency of Fantasy is to avoid truth, to be satisfied with a relation to the world consisting of arbitrary, subjective pictures. But now, from the dreamlike, enchanted summer-experience he had acquired insight which enabled him to say: Whatever rises up in me as creative fantasy I can carry out into the world. Out of my inner being, like the pictures of fantasy, grow the Imaginations of the plants. If I have fantasy pictures only, then I am a stranger to what is around me. But if I have Imaginations, there grows out of my own inner self everything that I can find in this plant, in that plant, in this animal, in this man, in that man. . . ." [90]

This is the answer to this fundamental question: to escape inner isolation, solitude's lie, the subjectivity of my creating of images, I must have the courage to carry what is born of my creative fantasy, this world of interior images, into the world. How differently now do the brilliant lines and shining images of "Pan" appear!

> If you have, alive and pressing,
> An inner world of images in you,
> Of thoughts, feelings, love, and burning passions,
> To impregnate the world, exchange it unceasingly
> For the other, visible world that closes in upon us!
> Mix your whole soul with creation!

Everything becomes clearer, grounded in a profound knowledge of the human soul. The sublime words by which Hugo in his poetic experience rediscovers — over the centuries — what still resonates in his soul as initiatory experience — do not these words now sound forth more distinctly? Steiner writes: "Feeling his relationship with the landscapes of winter and summer, the aspirant had acquired a clear idea both of nature and of himself, and he felt deeply united with outer nature and with his own being. . . . At the end he had to come to a clear realization of that state in which he felt himself spread out, and as if dispersed, in the world of the senses."

O sacred poets, wild, sublime,
Go, spread your souls upon the peaks.

Such are the experiences that the candidate for initiation really underwent. Creative fantasy?

If you have, alive and pressing,
An inner world of images in you,
Of thoughts, feelings, love, and burning passions, . . .

The disciple of the Hibernian Mysteries felt himself as if spread out in the world of the senses:

To impregnate the world, exchange it unceasingly. . . .

Steiner: The aspirant "felt himself deeply united with outer nature."

Mix your whole soul with creation. . . .

Here we see explained, in all its complexity, the crucial question of form and content. Empty form — true, clear, but without content; living substance, active but without form or clarity, capable of leading to error and lies. The Hibernian Initiation, by means of the experience of the two statues, led to the solution of this existential dilemma. And Hugo felt rising in him impulses towards this solution. Did not one critic intuitively characterize Hugo with this lapidary phrase: "Victor Hugo is a form who one day went out in search of his content, and finally found it." [91]

Seen from another perspective, the initiation experience conveys the relation of microcosm to macrocosm. As Steiner says of the Hibernian Mysteries: "One learned to know one-self in them as a microcosm, that is, as a being related physically, psychically and spiritually to the macrocosm. . . . Truly these Mysteries are great Mysteries. . . ."

To close, let us quote from "Pan" a verse that should leave no doubt as to this poem's initiatory origin. Recall the passage cited earlier that describes the images of summer and winter that rose up in the soul of the pupil of the Hibernian Mysteries. Before the male statue, the pupil was led "to an experience of the annihilation of his being accompanied by dreams of winter"; before the female statue, "the experience was accompanied by a summer dream." Now listen to the poet:

> Go into the forests, go into the vales,
> Perform a concert of isolated notes!
> Seek nature spread out before your eyes,
> Whether winter saddens or summer gladdens
> The mysterious word which each voice stammers,
> Hear what the thunder speaks in the skies.

NOTES

The Fragments of Novalis may be found in German in Novalis, *Werke*, Band 2, Carl Hanser Verlag, Munich and Vienna, 1978. The most complete collection in English is: Novalis, *Pollen and Fragments*, translated and introduced by Arthur Versluis, Phanes Press, Grand Rapids, 1989.

1. Rudolf Steiner, *Karmic Relationships*, vol. 1, lecture of 2/17/24, Rudolf Steiner Press, London, 1981.

2. Ibid, lecture of 1/24/24.

3. Rudolf Steiner, *The Work of the Angels in Man's Astral Body*, Lecture of 10/9/18, Rudolf Steiner Press, London, 1988.

4. Rudolf Steiner, *The Last Address*, Rudolf Steiner Press, London, 1967.

5. See note 3.

6. Ibid.

7. See note 2.

8. Rudolf Steiner, *Awakening to Community*, lecture of 2/27/23, Anthroposophic Press, Spring Valley, 1974.

9. Rudolf Steiner, *The Challenge of the Times*, Lecture of 12/7/18, Anthroposophic Press, Hudson, n.d.

10. Wooden group sculpture ("The Representative of Humanity"), sculpted by Rudolf Steiner and Edith Maryon, representing Christ between Lucifer and Ahriman. The scup1ture may be seen in the Goetheanum in Dornach, Switzerland.

11. See note 1.

12. Ibid.

13. Rudolf Steiner, *The Mission of the Archangel Michael*, Lecture of 11/23/19, Anthroposophic Press, Hudson .

14. Rudolf Steiner, *The Inner Aspect of the Social Question*, lecture of 2/11/19, Rudolf Steiner Press, London, 1974.

15. Rudolf Steiner, *Karmic Relationships*, vol. 2, lecture of 5/9/24, Rudolf Steiner Press, London, 1974.

16. Ita Wegman, *To the Friends: Transactions and Reports from 1925-27*. 2nd ed., Natura Verlag, Arlesheim, 1968. Not translated. This passage dates from 6/7/25.

17. See Rudolf Steiner, *The Christmas Conference for the Foundation of the General Anthroposophical Society 1923/1924*, Anthroposophic Press, Hudson, 1990.

18. See note 16.

19. *Knowledge of Higher Worlds and Its Attainment*, Anthroposophic Press, Spring Valley, 1983.

20. See note 3.

21. Ernst Lehrs, *Gelebte Erwartung*, J.C. Mellinger Verlag, Stuttgart, 1979. The translation of the Foundation Stone given here attempts to be true both to the French of Athys Floride and to the original German. For other translations by Michael Wilson, George Adams, Arvia MacKaye Ege, and Richard Seddon, see *The Christmas Conference* (note 17 above).

22. Rudolf Steiner, *Occult History*, lecture of 12/30/10, Rudolf Steiner Press, London, 1982.

23. See note 2.

24. Ibid.

25. Rudolf Steiner, *The Easter Festival in the Evolution of the Mysteries*, lecture of 4/19/24, Anthroposophic Press, Hudson, 1988.

26. Ibid.

27. Ibid., lecture of 7/21/24.

28. C.f. Emil Funk, *Calendar for 1913–14: An Initiative of Rudolf Steiner*, Dornach 1973 (not translated).

29. See note 27.

30. Rudolf Steiner, *Man and the World of Stars* (including *The Spiritual Communion of Humanity*), lecture of 12/24/22, Anthroposophic Press, Spring Valley, 1982.

31. Ibid.

32. Orally transmitted by Friedrich Rittelmeyer.

33. See note 17, lecture of 12/25/23.

34. The four stages in a human encounter can be seen as corresponding to stages of higher cognition. Cf. Rudolf Steiner,

Stages of Higher Knowledge, Anthroposophic Press, Hudson, 1990.

35. See note 3.

36. Rudolf Steiner, *The Mission of Folk Souls*, Rudolf Steiner Press, London.

37. Ibid.

38. See note 1, lecture of 3/2/24.

39. See note 8.

40. Ibid.

41. *Wir Erlebten Rudolf Steiner*, edited by M. J. Kruck von Poturzyn, 6th ed., Stuttgart 1980 (not translated).

42. Ibid.

43. Rudolf Steiner, *Human and Cosmic Thought*, lecture of 1/23/14, Rudolf Steiner Press, London, n.d.

44. Rudolf Steiner, Marie Steiner, *Correspondence and Documents 1901-1925*, Anthroposophic Press, Hudson, 1988.

45. Rudolf Steiner, *Karmic Relationships*, vol. V, lecture of 25/5/24; also vol. VII, lecture of 10/6/24; Rudolf Steiner Press, London 1986 and 1973.

46. Rudolf Steiner, *Karmic Relationships* vols. I, II, III, IV, V, VI, VII, VIII, Rudolf Steiner Press, London, various dates.

47. Rudolf Steiner, *Theosophy*, Anthroposophic Press, Hudson, 1988.

48. See note 22.

49. See note 15.

50. Rudolf Steiner, *Mystery Knowledge and Mystery Centres*, Rudolf Steiner Press, London, 1973.

51. C.f. Victor Hugo, *Oeuvres poétiques complètes*, Jean Jacques Pauvert, Paris, 1961. All translations have been made from this edition.

52. The first part was published in German in the *Blätter für Anthroposophie* in May 1965 on the occasion of the eighty-fifth anniversary of the poet's death.

53. In an article in the *Figaro* 11/5/1945

54. Quoted by Henri Guillemin in *Victor Hugo par lui-meme*, Edition du Seuil, Paris, 1959.

55. Charles Baudelaire, *L'Art romantique*.

56. see note 45.

57. Ibid.

58. Charles Baudelaire, *Oeuvres complètes*, Club du Livre, Paris, n.d.

59. Fernard Gregh, *L'Oeuvre de Victor Hugo*, Flammarion, Paris, 1933.

60. Alain — source unknown.

61. André Maurois, *Olympio ou La Vie de Victor Hugo*, Hachette, Paris, 1954.

62. See note 45.

63. Ibid.

64. See note 54.

65. L. Mabilleau, *Victor Hugo*

66. C.f Novalis, *The Hymns to the Night*. For Novalis, like Hugo, the sun is to be found at night.

67. Rudolf Steiner, *Colour*, lecture of 12/5/20, Rudolf Steiner Press, London, 1935.

68. Ibid.

69. *Dernière Gerbe* ("Last Sheaf"), November 26, 1876. Hugo was seventy-six years of age and seems to have overcome fear, as the first stanza affirms.

70. Rudolf Steiner, *The Guardian of the Threshold*, in *Four Mystery Dramas*, Steiner Book Centre, Vancouver, 1978, now Anthroposophic Press, Hudson.

71. Book of Revelation, 1: 16-17.

72. See note 45.

73. Bhagavad Gita XI, 8, 24, 25, 31, 32. Adapted from Penguin edition (translated by Juan Mascaro), Harmondsworth, 1962.

74. *La Légende des Siècles* ("The Legend of the Centuries"), "Plein Ciel" ("Open Sky").

75. Quoted by Guillemin, op. cit. (See note 54).

76. In a letter to Louise Colet, June 1, 1854, he calls himself a "citizen of heaven." Quoted by Guillemin (see note 54).

77. *Essai sur l'Ecole romantique*, Nisard, Paris, n.d.

78. *Figaro*, June 13, 1883.

79. see note 54.

80. see note 58.

81. A. Houssaye, *Confession* (no additional information).

82. *Les Feuilles d'Automne* ("Autumn Leaves"); "Ce Siècle avait deux ans" ("The century was two years old").

83. See note 50.

84. See note 55.

85. See note 50.

86. *Les Feuilles d'Automne* ("Autumn Leaves"), "Ce que dit la bouche d'ombre" ("What the mouth of the shadow says").

87. See note 50.

88. *Les Feuilles d'Automne* ("Autumn Leaves"), "Pan."

89. See 50.

90. Ibid.

91. Claude Roy.

ACKNOWLEDGMENTS

We would like to thank the Collegium of the Social Science Section of the School of Spiritual Science in the United States for bringing this book to our attention; and Catherine Creeger who made a first translation for the Social Science Section from the German version entitled *Die Begegnung als Aufwacherlebnis* (*Encounter as Resurrection Experience*).

As it turned out, this version was both different textually from the French and incomplete. It did not contain the second half of the French text on "Encountering a poet through his work." This naturally caused a quandary until Athys Floride, the author, confirmed that the French text was primary. In the ensuing process of revision and retranslation Catherine Creeger's original version gradually disappeared. Nevertheless, we would like to acknowledge her work here.

About the Author

Athys Aimé Floride was born April 15, 1924, in Cayenne, French Guyana. He was trained as a figher pilot in North Africa at the end of World War II; by the end of 1945, he was in occupied Germany in the French zone (near Lake Constance). From 1946 to 1952, he was in Paris, studying philosophy at the Sorbonne and ethnology at the Faculté des Sciences de Paris (Musée de l'Homme). He was then a teacher of philosophy at various French schools and colleges. In 1956–58 he helped in the founding of the Waldorf Movement in France. In 1958, he went to Germany as teacher of languages in Benefeld. He returned to France in 1965 for the founding of an institute for curative education (St. Martin in Normandy) where he worked for a few months. At the end of 1965 he moved back to Germany to teach in the Waldorf School in Kassel, from which he became a language consultant for the German Waldorf Schools. From 1970–80 he was a member of the Board of the Anthroposophical Center in Frankfurt-am-Main. Since 1982, he has been a member of the Board of the Anthroposophical Society in France.

RECOVERING THE SOURCES OF MEANING: THE PATH OF ANTHROPOSOPHY

Anthroposophy, which means "the wisdom of the human being," is not just an abstract philosophy but a living spiritual path that reconnects human beings to the universe and to the sources of what it means to be human. Rudolf Steiner, who renewed this path of meaning in our time, saw four of his books as fundamental to the recovery of human dignity. Despite the many other books he wrote and the more than 6,000 lectures he gave, Steiner returned again and again to these four basic books.

The Basic Books

The Philosophy of Spiritual Activity

This fundamental work of philosophy demonstrates the fact of freedom — the ability to think and act independently — as a possibility for modern consciousness. Read properly, the book leads the reader to experience the living thinking by which all human activity may be renewed.

Knowledge of Higher Worlds and its Attainment

This is the fundamental guide to the anthroposophical path of knowledge. In human consciousness faculties sleep that, if awoken, lead to life-giving wisdom. With great clarity and warmth Steiner details the exercises and moral qualities to be cultivated on the path to conscious experience of supersensible realities.

Theosophy

This work, subtitled "An Introduction to the Supersensible Knowledge of the World and Human Destiny," begins by describing the threefold nature of the human being: the body or sense-world, the soul or inner world, the spirit or universal world of cosmic archetypes. A profound discussion of reincarnation and karma follows, concluding with a description of the soul's journey through the supersensible regions after death. The book closes with an outline of the path to higher knowledge.

An Outline of Occult Science

This masterwork of esotericism places humanity at the heart of the vast, invisible processes of cosmic evolution. Descriptions of the different members of the human being, in themselves and in relation to sleep and death, are followed by a profound investigation of cosmic evolution and the beings that direct it. The book concludes with a detailed, practical guide to the methods by which such "initiation" knowledge may be attained.

Related titles

Christianity as Mystical Fact

Christianity arose out of what was prepared in the pre-Christian Mysteries. However, Christianity was not merely a further development of what existed in these Mysteries but something unique and independent. Against this background, the book includes discussions of the Gospels, the raising of Lazarus, the Apocalypse, and the historical background of Jesus.

The Christmas Conference 1923/24

The Laying of the Foundation Stone in the hearts of the assembled members forms the center of this elegant and beautiful book that documents the founding of the General Anthroposophical Society. The Foundation Stone Mantra is reproduced in the form that Rudolf Steiner gave it on each day of the Conference, together with his comments on the mantra's various rhythms.

Four Mystery Dramas

These four plays, depicting the experiences of a group of people and their relationships as they go on a path of spiritual development, contain the essence of anthroposophy.

The Calendar of the Soul

Steiner's fifty-two meditative verses help one to participate actively in the life of the year as it unfolds week by week.

The Course of My Life

This is Steiner's remarkable autobiography in which he traces his life through his forty-sixth year. Rather than focussing on outer events, he describes the path of his soul development and the struggles he went through to develop his world view.

Other authors

Water: The Element of Life
by Theodor and Wolfram Schwenk

This outstanding collection of essays by the author of *Sensitive Chaos* and his son ranges over a wide range of topics from the cosmic significance of water to its behavior and nutritive value. Above all, the authors convincingly depict the earth as a living organism, with water as its sense organ, perceiving cosmic life-giving forces and allowing them to enter our earthly realm. As the authors explain, it is the living movement of water that makes life on earth possible. Their solutions for the current water and ecological crises go beyond piecemeal measures to a comprehensive and radical "water consciousness."

Encountering the Self: Transformation and Destiny in the Ninth Year
by Hermann Koepke

The author, a Waldorf teacher of many years experience, provides a lucid explanation of the events occurring in the life of a child between the ninth and the tenth year. This is the time when the child's I incarnates more deeply. As a result, children at this age experience themselves for the first time as separate individuals, an experience often accompanied by a first encounter with death, a first inkling that life is fragile and does not go on forever.

*The Golden Age of Chartres: The Teachings of the
Mystery School and the Eternal Feminine*
by Rene Querido

Here is the fascinating history of Chartres up to the Golden
Age when the Cathedral was built on the site where Druids had
worshipped the sun. Following a historical survey, Querido
unfolds the meaning of the statues and images of the Cathedral
and then turns to the four best known teachers of the famous
School of Chartres. The final chapters deal with the intricate
working together of Platonic and Aristotelian influences in our
time.

Toward the Twenty-First Century
Bernard Lievegoed

This book presents many esoteric facets of the spiritual drama
behind the events of the twentieth century and indicates how
the human being can act within this context to further the good.

For prices and a catalogue of titles published and distributed
by Anthroposophic Press, please write to:

Anthroposophic Press
RR4, Box 94 A-1,
Hudson, New York 12534
Telephone: 518-851-2054